HIGH
PERFORMANCE
SALES
ORGANIZATIONS

HIGH PERFORMANCE SALES ORGANIZATIONS

Achieving Competitive Advantage in the Global Marketplace

Second Edition

Darlene M. Coker

Edward R. Del Gaizo, Ph.D.

Kathleen A. Murray

Sandra L. Edwards

New York   San Francisco   Washington, D.C.   Auckland   Bogotá
Caracas   Lisbon   London   Madrid   Mexico City   Milan   Montreal
New Delhi   San Juan   Singapore   Sydney   Tokyo   Toronto

McGraw-Hill

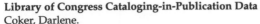

A Division of The McGraw-Hill Companies

Library of Congress Cataloging-in-Publication Data
Coker, Darlene.
   High performance sales organizations: creating competitive
advantage in the global marketplace.--2nd ed. / by Darlene Coker,
Edward R. Del Gaizo, Kathleen A. Murray, Sandra L. Edwards.
      p.   cm.
   Rev. ed. of: High performance sales organizations / Kevin J.
Corcoran ... [et al.]. c1995.
   Includes biblioographical references and index.
   ISBN 0-07-135160-4
   1. Sales management.   2. Selling.   3. Customer relations.
I. Del Gaizo, Edward R.   II. Murray, Kathleen A.   Edwards, Sandra L.
III. High performance sales organizations.   IV. Title.
HF5438.4.H54   1998   99-37629
658.8'1--dc21   CIP

2 3 4 5 6 7 8 9 0 DOC/DOC 0 9 8 7 6 5 4 3 2 1 0

ISBN 0-07-135160-4

The sponsoring editor for this book was Jeffrey Krames, the editing supervisor was John M. Morriss, and the production supervisor was Elizabeth J. Strange.

Printed and bound by R. R. Donnelley & Sons Company.

McGraw-Hill books are available at special quantity discounts to use as premiums and sales promotions, or for use in corporate training programs. For more information, please write to the Director of Special Sales, McGraw-Hill, Professional Publishing, Two Penn Plaza, New York, NY 10121-2298. Or contact your local bookstore.

This publication is designed to provide accurate and authoritative information in regard to the subject matter covered. It is sold with the understanding that neither the author nor the publisher is engaged in rendering legal, accounting, or other professional service. If legal advice or other expert assistance is required, the services of a competent professional person should be sought.
—*From a Declaration of Principles jointly adopted by a Committee of the American Bar Association and a Committee of Publishers.*

 This book is printed on recycled, acid-free paper containing a minimum of 50% recycled, de-inked fiber.

Foreword

by Ron Zemke

For most of the last decade, the focus of business has been everything but selling. Branding. Positioning. Quality. Innovation. Globalization. Internet. Technology. As important as those ideas are to a business, none of them has the immediacy and impact on an organization's fate as does the ageless act of selling; going out, finding a prospect, and turning that prospect into a customer—someone who buys and uses, repurchases, and reuses, your company's products and services time and again.

Make no mistake, selling today—particularly business-to-business selling—is inordinately more complex and demanding than it was a decade ago, or just five years ago, or just last year. It is no longer a simple "feet-in-street" or "sales calls per day," activity-based craft.

Selling today, more than ever, means finding the right prospect, learning everything you can about the prospect's needs, and being skilled at demonstrating how you and your products and services can fill those needs. Mark Bozzini, CEO of Linkexchange, Inc., in San Francisco, put it as succinctly as I've ever seen it in a recent *Fast Company* article: "Clients don't care about your stuff. They care about their stuff." To which I can only add: **A-men!**

And selling today more than ever is about building relationships that last. Frederick Reichheld, author of the 1993 best seller *The Loyalty Effect,* points out a 5-percentage point advantage in customer retention is equal to doubling your number of customers every fourteen years. That long-term customer, the customer turned partner, is the most valuable asset a company can have. Key to the conversion from end-user to partner is a salesperson empowered, trained, and rewarded for managing long-term relationships and for turning customership into true partnership.

Darlene Coker, Ed Del Gaizo, Kate Murray, and Sandra Edwards, the authors of *High Performance Sales Organizations,* have not only catalogued these and a plethora of other mission-critical issues that impact today's sales organization; they provide proven pathways for dealing with and mastering them. Their best practices research on these issues is superb!

Whether you are looking for help defining and explaining today's customer to your salespeople, evaluating sales support technology, or simply searching for a leg up on managing and coaching the "new" sales workforce, you'll find aid and comfort here. If that's not enough, the authors provide a tantalizing look at what selling in the first decades of the new century will—might—could—look like.

Small wonder it took four people to write this book. There is four times more information packed into *High Performance Sales Organizations* than you'll find in a dozen "normal," selling and sales management tomes.

Fortunately, you don't need a zip drive or an un-zip program to get at it. Just turn the page and dive in!

Ron Zemke

Coauthor of *Service America: Doing Business in the New Economy*

and

The *Knock Your Socks Off Service* Series

Contents

Acknowledgments

AchieveGlobal's research studies and experiences with sales organizations around the world provided the underlying ideas for both the original and revised versions of this book. We appreciate these sales organizations' willingness to share their ideas and their candor about the issues they face.

Howard Kamens was an enormous contributor to the book, as our technology expert and as a steadfast moral supporter. He will always be a friend to AchieveGlobal and a contributor to the field of sales performance and training.

Mark ter Haar managed the Sales Leadership research project in Europe, and Shigetaka Takeuchi, Hideo Yamanan, and their team at Fuji Xerox Learning Institute managed the Sales Leadership research in Japan. They provided many ideas that shaped the original thinking for the book.

The revision process would not have been possible if not for the efforts of Angie Nicholson, Audrey Ellison, Beth Potter, Bruce Phillipson, Christina Muth, Corinne Mason, Craig Topp, Dale Arnold, Denese Schmelzkopf, Ed Ness, James Fennessey, Joe Wozniak, John Guziak, Juan Gutierrez, Kathy Bunch, Kristin Barton, Lisa Fagan, Luke McNally, Marcia Heath, Mark Marone, Martha Chamberlain, Maureen Kelly, Niko Siopis, Polly Thompson, Rowena Row, Sarah Porter, Scott Sklares, Todd Szewczyk, Toni Sheppard, Zella DuToit, Charry Palmer, and Jan Birberick.

A special thank you to Jim King for his infinite patience and flexibility, to Marija Bryant for her talent and insight, to Kathy David for her work with Frontier and her ability to capture the story, to Alexandra Lang for her attention to detail and willingness to jump in on the project. And to Greger Berg, Leslie Aitken, Frank Ronault, Marc Van Dern Broeck, and Derwin Fox for their contributions of knowledge and understanding. Without these people, this book could not have been completed.

Jeffrey Krames, Laura Libretti, Kelly Christiansen and John Morriss at McGraw-Hill have been an enormous help, as well as Marlyss McPherson and Asha Knutsen at Advantage Research and Consulting. Many thanks also to Don Kitzmiller and Howard Stevens of H. R. Chally and Kevin Klivnex of Select International.

Thanks also to contributors Kim Kleps, Donna Reeves, Jeff Worth, and Brian Spanswick.

We would also like to thank the original authors and contributors for their work in laying the foundation for a living, dynamic book that will continue to improve the performance of sales professionals and organizations around the world.

About AchieveGlobal

AchieveGlobal, Inc., a division of the Times Mirror Company, is the world's largest provider of performance skills training and consulting. It represents the integration of three leaders in their respective fields: Kaset International in customer loyalty, Learning International in sales performance, and Zenger Miller in leadership and organizational effectiveness.

With nearly 1000 employees in 44 offices across North America, affiliate partners in more than 40 countries, and training in more than 40 languages and dialects, AchieveGlobal serves more than 400 of the *Fortune* 500 companies and more than 300 of the *Canadian Financial Post* 500 companies. You can learn more about AchieveGlobal and its products and services on its web site at *www.achieveglobal.com* or by calling 800-456-9390.

"The definition of competition has unmasked its new appearance since the manufacturing and quality-centered focus in the past. The role has evolved to meet the new demands and challenges related to information networking and IT-centered focus and stand in the spotlight of Mega Competition within a global marketplace. How one should act in this competitive arena is the fundamental question that is raised.

This book directs this fundamental theme raised by corporate players and communicates fresh hints for success in how corporations should cast their marketing functions to the front-line to identify the market and clients. Also, this book examines the factors leading to successful long-term business relationships, and overall skills to achieve an encore of high performance."

Yotaro Kobayashi
Chairman of the Board,
Fuji Xerox Co., Ltd

I

MARKET DYNAMICS

"I expect a salesperson to be a professional business person who happens to be involved in selling."

Chapter One

In Pursuit of Loyal Customer Partners

"If you have a strong relationship with a salesperson, you can live through the pricing problems, you can live through the delivery problems, you can live through anything—as long as you can trust each other."

—Customer, 3M (United Kingdom)

- What are the differences between loyal partners and satisfied customers?
- Are the differences important?
- What do customers expect from sales organizations?
- Are sales organizations meeting the most important expectations of their customers?

Faced with demanding customers and aggressive competitors, sales executives around the world confront this question every day: "What can we do to gain loyal customer partners and improve our own profitability in a fiercely competitive market?"

Leading sales executives say that long-term relationships are critical to the success of their organizations. In fact, nearly every one of the thousands of sales organizations AchieveGlobal has worked with in the past several years has emphasized the importance of building partnerships with loyal customers.

Partners

Two or more people or organizations working together toward a mutually beneficial common goal with loyalty and a long-term commitment to each other's success.

Why is partnership with customers so important? First, because partners are an excellent source of referrals. More importantly though, long-term, mutually beneficial relationships are more profitable for most sales organizations because of the costs associated with starting up a business relationship. Evidence to support this notion has been mounting over the years. As far back as 1990, Fredrick Reichheld and W. Earl Sasser, Jr., showed that a 5 percent increase in customer retention could yield anywhere between a 20 to 100 percent increase in profitability.[1] A true customer-supplier partnership is the epitome of customer loyalty.

A survey of U.S. sales organizations jointly conducted by *Sales & Marketing Management* magazine and Personnel Corporation of America in 1990 also confirmed the importance of long-term relationships.[2] It suggested that profit margins from new accounts are often much lower than those for subsequent sales. In fact, it took an average of seven sales calls to close a first sale to a new customer; in contrast, it took only three calls to close a subsequent sale with an *existing* customer.

This finding is even more important in light of the continually increasing cost of sales calls. The same study concluded that the average cost of a business-to-business sales call was increasing at an alarming rate. Long-term relationships generally may be more profitable, but the "profit" can't be taken for granted. By making too many concessions to long-term customers, or by erroneously assuming that long-term customers are also loyal partners, a sales organization can end up with long-term but extremely unprofitable relationships. To have a true partnership, the relationship has to be

---

[1]Fredrick F. Reichheld and W. Earl Sasser, Jr., "Zero Defections: Quality Comes to Service," *Harvard Business Review,* (September–October 1990).

[2]William A. O'Connell and William Keenan, Jr., "The Shape of Things to Come," *Sales & Marketing Management* (January 1990), p. 38.

Loyal Customer

A buyer who chooses to do business with a particular supplier and commits to buy from that supplier in the future.

Satisfied Customer

A buyer who buys from a particular supplier, but expects to buy from others in the future.

---

mutual. Often customers use the word *partnership*, but the relationship only benefits them, leaving the supplier to make all of the concessions and take on all of the risk.

Add to this ever-increasing challenge the concept of growth. Not only are companies charged with cutting costs, at the same time they are expected to grow in the face of increasing competition. Reichheld ties this concept to customer loyalty as well: "Other things being equal, a 5 percentage point advantage in customer retention translates into a growth advantage equal to a doubling of customer inventory every 14 years. An advantage of 10 percentage points accelerates the doubling to seven years."[3]

The challenge that sales executives face every day is how to make trade-offs between these goals—how to invest in developing long-term customer partnerships while achieving targets for growth and profitability.

A MISUNDERSTOOD NOTION

Achieving partnerships through customer loyalty is a job that's never done. Because customers are continually changing, the factors on which they evaluate sales organizations are changing also. And the bar is continually being raised; their expectations are continually going up. Today's added value is tomorrow's expected value.

A satisfied customer buys from a particular supplier, but expects to buy from others in the future. That's one reason we're all still striving for customer loyalty after years of focusing on customer

---

[3]Frederick F. Reichheld, *The Loyalty Effect* (Boston: Harvard Business School Press, 1996), p. 37.

satisfaction, enhancing quality, streamlining processes, and getting closer to customers. One only has to look at large U.S. long-distance providers—AT&T, Sprint, and MCI—for an example. As products and services become harder to distinguish, a customer who is satisfied with one supplier in the morning can be snatched away by another by the end of the same business day. Customer loyalty is elusive: it is a valiant objective, but not a permanent state.

One reason is that the speed of product innovation and time to market is increasing. And some companies are competing with businesses that are outside their industry. Union Pacific Railroad, for example, has to compete not only with other rail transporters but also with those outside their business, including barge services and trucking companies.

Another reason that customer loyalty is hard to sustain is because it is difficult to know whether a customer is really loyal or merely satisfied. Sales organizations often assume that a repeat customer is a loyal customer. In fact, on closer examination, he or she may only be a satisfied customer—and susceptible to offers from the competition of better prices and more value. These customers are not loyal, and as such they are not likely to become true partners.

It is important to distinguish between loyal customers, those with whom we can have a partnership, and satisfied customers. Why? Because the sales organizations that succeed in the future will be the ones that segment their markets and have strategies for meeting the needs of each segment profitably. The investments they make—in resources, services, time, and concessions—to achieve their goals with each segment will be deliberate decisions made in the context of those strategies, with a focus on their own profitability.

THE QUEST FOR PROFITABLE CUSTOMER PARTNERSHIPS

Presumably, all organizations would like to ensure that their salespeople satisfy customers and build profitable business partnerships with them—"a profitable working relationship characterized by a 'win-win' approach," as a sales manager from Boehme Chemie (Germany) described it. But not only is it unfortunate to lose the right customers, it is a mistake to *keep* the wrong customers. As most of us know, trying to satisfy *every* customer request is becoming both more expensive and painfully unprofitable.

Also, while customer retention can certainly contribute to growth, the concept that *any* customer retention will translate into profitable growth is just as inaccurate. As Christopher Fay of the Juran Institute points out, "simply retaining a customer in no way ensures, or even heightens, the customer's loyalty." He cites an example of a computer hardware company that boasted of retaining its customer base only to find, on closer examination, that one reason its profits were not soaring was that more than half of its "loyal" customers had gone on to purchase add-ons and services from the competition.[4]

Sales executives and directors know how important profitability is, but salespeople frequently don't think about whether they're developing *profitable* customer partnerships. Usually, their primary concern is to bring in revenue. This is understandable, given that their compensation is often based solely on meeting revenue targets. As shown in AchieveGlobal's 1990 sales force study, about half (52 percent) the sales executives interviewed said that their sales forces' goals were based simply on revenues, without taking profits into consideration.[5] Today, this situation hasn't changed much. Many organizations still struggle to track costs and assign accurate profitability measures to the sales process, so compensation continues to be based on revenue volume.

Those that have been able to institute a profit-based system see the rewards. At Castrol Industrial North America's Performance Lubricants division, salespeople are paid 100-percent commission based on profit margin. In this way, their performance and reward structure are directly linked to the company's success, not just volume.

By linking the concepts of pay for performance with profit and customer loyalty, organizations are able to enter knowledgeably into true partnerships that benefit all concerned: the customer, the sales organization, and the salesperson.

BEST PRACTICES FROM GLOBAL SALES LEADERS

AchieveGlobal decided that if anyone *did* have clues about developing a profitable customer partnership, they would be leading sales

---

[4]Christopher Fay, "Royalties from Loyalties," *Journal of Business Strategy* 15, no. 2 (March/April 1994), pp. 47–51.

[5]AchieveGlobal, "Sales Productivity in the 1990s," Preliminary Report (1990), p. 9.

organizations. We developed a research study to profile them and selected 24 sales leaders around the world. (See Appendix A.) Each is highly regarded within its market and industry and offers strong products and services, leading-edge research, and efficient operations. These assets certainly contribute to their customers' loyalty.

Yet, these organizations have another idea about what it takes to stay competitive. What these organizations have in common is that they are challenging themselves to define what their salespeople will have to do differently to differentiate their organizations through the quality and durability of the relationships they build with their customers.

"When products and services are virtually identical, the differentiator is the salesperson and his or her management of the customer relationship," observed the vice president for marketing at American Airlines (United States).

The leading sales organizations we studied have demonstrated that they have what it takes to succeed today, and what they say about succeeding in the future is this: Success will belong to those organizations that ensure that their salespeople build lasting *business partnerships* with loyal customers. The keys to this are building credibility, knowing what their customers want, and meeting—or exceeding—their expectations.

GREAT EXPECTATIONS

What is it that customers expect from suppliers? In a series of studies on customer loyalty, AchieveGlobal examined the key factors that influence a customer's decision to stay with a supplier. Business-to-business customers from a wide variety of industries in 13 countries were surveyed. Each customer was asked to provide ratings to indicate the extent to which each of 63 statements *should* describe their suppliers.[6] Participants were also asked to rate the extent to which the statements *actually* describe a current supplier. Comparisons between "should" and "actual" ratings revealed unmet, met, and exceeded expectations.

---

[6]AchieveGlobal, *Profiles in Customer Loyalty*, 1989, and *Achieving Customer Loyalty in Europe*, 1992. For a complete listing of the expectations analyzed in the Customer Loyalty Research, see Appendix C.

The study suggested that the six expectations listed in Table 1-1 rank highest in three major world markets—North America, Europe, and Japan.

This list of top expectations strikes at some very basic aspects of doing business. That might be predictable. But notice that five of the expectations depend on either the *salesperson's* actual performance or the expectations that he or she creates about the supplier organization and its products or services. This is very revealing. What was profoundly startling was that in all three markets most of these key expectations are unmet (see Table 1-2). Specifically:

- In North America, three of these expectations were met, but not exceeded, by suppliers: a salesperson's honesty, product and service quality and an organization that can be trusted.

- In Europe, only one expectation was met: an organization that can be trusted.

- In Japan, supplier performance falls short of customers' expectations in all areas.

Presumably, a supplier's ability, and a customer's willingness, to develop a strong partnership depends largely on how well the supplier satisfies the customer's most basic expectations. For instance, a supplier who doesn't deliver a product on time shouldn't expect a customer to look to him to address higher-level needs, such as problem-solving assistance.

On the other hand, a supplier that consistently meets these basic needs has the freedom to differentiate through other, less conventional offerings. (See Figure 1-1.)

So what does the customer want? In the long run, everything. But what the customer wants now depends on what satisfaction level is

TABLE 1-1
Highest Expectations in North America, Europe, and Japan

A supplier organization that can be trusted
A salesperson who is honest
A salesperson who keeps promises
A product or service that is delivered on time
A product or service that is consistent in quality
A product or service that performs as anticipated

A supplier organization that can be trusted
A salesperson who is honest
A salesperson who keeps promises
A product or service that is delivered on time
A product or service that is consistent in quality
A product or service that performs as anticipated

TABLE 1-2
Are Highest Expectations Being Met?

Expectations that Rank High in North America, Europe, and Japan	Unmet, Met, and Exceeded Expectations		
	North America	Europe	Japan
A supplier organization that can be trusted	Met	Met	Unmet
A salesperson who is honest	Met	Unmet	Unmet
A salesperson who keeps promises	Unmet	Unmet	Unmet
A product or service that is delivered on time	Unmet	Unmet	Unmet
A product or service that is consistent in quality	Met	Unmet	Unmet
A product or service that performs as anticipated	Unmet	Unmet	Unmet

currently being met. By meeting these customer needs sequentially and cumulatively, ultimately you give the customer everything, and become a partner on the inside, rather than a suitor on the outside.[7]

Yet, the results of the research strongly suggest that many organizations have difficulty meeting even customers' most important expectations. (See Tables 1-1 and 1-2.) Given this finding, it is not surprising that so many companies find it extraordinarily difficult to turn the ideal of profitable customer partnerships into a reality. Most are still grappling with the basics—making promises they can fulfill; delivering a consistent, quality product on time; demonstrating integrity; and establishing trust. It appears that any sales or-

---

[7]Mike Herrington, "What Does a Customer Want?" *Across the Board* (April 1993).

FIGURE 1–1
Hierarchy of Customer Expectations

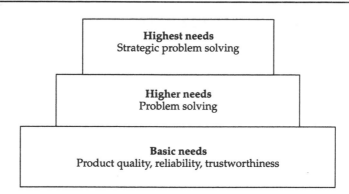

ganization that is serious about competing virtually anywhere in the industrialized world must focus on these basic expectations.

START AT THE BEGINNING

All indications point to the sales organization's role in achieving more enduring and more profitable business partnerships as increasingly important. But where do you start?

- Look at your customer base. Identify those who are loyal customers and those who fall in other categories.
- Focus on improving your relationships with those who have the potential to become profitable, long-term partners.
- Understand how your customers are changing and how your sales force is changing. After all, the changes you make in your sales organization should ultimately link back to your customers.
- Search for best practices from other companies, starting with companies that have distinguished themselves in their own markets. Look across boundaries into areas you may not have previously considered.

When we interviewed sales leaders and their customers in North America, Europe, and the Pacific Rim, we found that what they have in common is that they are focusing on understanding and working with a new type of customer—and developing their salespeople's ability to sell in a consultative manner.

Chapter Two

A New Type of Customer

*"If you think your relationship with the customer is nothing but a mat-
ter of buying and selling, that relationship will go nowhere. The relationship develops from additional activities that go beyond buying and
selling."*

—Salesperson, Fuji Xerox Co. (Japan)

- How are today's customers different?
- What do customers expect of salespeople?
- How are customer-supplier relationships evolving?
- What kind of strategy can build profitable business relation-
  ships?

You see it in the faces of your salespeople after long days on the
road, and you see it in their performance. They're struggling to
keep pace with a new type of customer. Not long ago, customers
might have been satisfied with a fair price and a good quality
product. Today, they demand a host of additional attributes—con-
venience of purchase, electronic data interface, after-sale support,
and customization services, to name a few. Not long ago, customers could have been swayed by the salesperson's affability and
social skills. Today, they are more influenced by the salesperson's
professionalism and business acumen.

What do these new customers look like? What is causing them to
be so much more demanding?

1. *Today's customers are more knowledgeable.* The past few years of
   rapid economic expansion, particularly in North America,
   has created a fluid job-market within and outside of many

organizations. Individuals are bringing more to the table in terms of experience and expectations. As a result, many of them are under pressure to quickly understand the impact of their purchase decisions on their business challenge and the company at large. Whole business thinking on the part of buyers is requiring more of the same from the salespeople they work with. A vice president at Bayerische Vereinsbank Group (Germany) commented on the typical customer's expanded base of knowledge, "Customers are more self-confident, and they know how to make use of their knowledge."

2. *Today's customers are more analytical.* Customers' buying decisions are more closely linked with key business strategies and require difficult choices about how best to use their organizations' limited resources. "Customers are very tough right now," said a sales manager for Xerox Corporation (United States). "They are more educated about business problems and the effect of their buying decisions on their P&Ls." As senior-level compensation models shift to reflect "shareholder value" and Wall Street scrutiny, pressures to manage the bottom line could not be more intense. Big-ticket or complex purchase decisions receive the most microscopic scrutiny, especially from high-level executives. Customers must be thoroughly analytical about all their purchase decisions, basing them solidly on the strengths of the supplier organizations' solutions and commitment.

3. *Today's customers are more demanding.* To respond to increased competition in their own markets, today's customers juggle more responsibilities with fewer resources and must, therefore, operate more efficiently and effectively. Because customers are pressed to do more with less, they are more determined than ever before to get good value for their investments. "My expectations are simple," commented a customer of Ordo (France). "I want the best possible service." Customers have a strong sense of entitlement, the result of the many options available to them as more suppliers compete for their business. This competition is heightened by the Internet as buyers easily can locate detailed product and service information from all the players competing in a marketplace, regardless of size and location. Said a sales manager from Rank Xerox (The Netherlands), "Clients have better insight about their options." As a salesperson for American Airlines (United States) said, "The travel agents who are my customers are dealing with 12 or 15 of my competitors. They

won't put all their eggs in one basket." The result?
Customers' expectations have soared. "We're expected to do
it all, at lower cost," reported a vice president of Hewlett-
Packard Company (United States).

4. *Today's customers provide more strategic information.* Today's
   customers expect more, but they are also willing to give
   more. In the interest of making the best purchase decisions
   for their organizations, more customers—especially in North
   America—are willing to share substantial information with
   the salespeople with whom they work.[1] As a vice president
   at Xerox Corporation (United States) observed, "There has
   been a major change in customers in that they are much
   more open in dealing with salespeople." As a result, sales
   conversations are more candid, and as a salesperson at Allen
   & Hanbury's (United Kingdom) noted, "Customers have a
   more positive attitude toward selling." Said a sales manager
   from Scott Paper Company (United States), "Salespeople and
   customers used to think of themselves as on opposite sides
   of the desk—as adversaries. Now there's more respect—
   more trust. We work together to develop the customer's
   business."

This increase in the information that is shared between suppliers
and customers symbolizes a radical change in business relationships at the most fundamental level. It reflects a new level of trust
and a new type of partnership. As more companies seek to move at
"Internet speed," trust and partnership become even more important than they have always been. If there is no time for recovery
from bad buying decisions, that does not mean that more time can
be allowed to make those decisions. In fact, the reverse is true; there
is less time, and that requires more trust and partnering to ensure
success.

---

[1]Learning International's white paper, *Achieving Customer Loyalty in Europe*
(1992), shows that customer-supplier relationships appear to be at various stages
of development, due to different political, economic, social, cultural, and competitive factors. For example, the four customer attributes just described are most
noticeable in the North American marketplace and less so in Europe and Japan.
As the European and Japanese markets become more open, supplier organizations are experiencing increasingly similar competitive pressures and escalating
customer expectations.

CUSTOMERS' EXPECTATIONS
OF SALESPEOPLE

"An ideal salesperson has a deep knowledge about his or her product and can recommend the best solution for a specific customer."

—Customer, Tokio Marine & Fire Insurance Company (Japan)

As markets become more competitive and customers become more so-phisticated, customers have *higher expectations of the salespeople with whom they do business.* They expect their suppliers' salespeople to rec-ommend solutions that will be focused on helping them compete more effectively. A sales manager with Iron Trades Insurance Group (United Kingdom) summed up the new expectation this way: "Customers are buying a concept as well as a product. They are looking for value for their money—and someone to make their business more profitable."

Equally important, they expect salespeople to exhibit the same high level of business knowledge and sophistication that they do. In the words of a vice president at Océ (The Netherlands), "The cus-tomer's expertise is growing, and he or she expects to work with a salesperson who can be considered an equal."

A customer of Scott Paper Company (United States) put it this way: "The level of competence demanded of salespeople will take quantum leaps. They need to be more clever, more professional, and have more technical knowledge because the customer base is more sophisticated about business." In addition, customers expect sales-people to perform the time-honored, customer-focused sales prac-tices more often and more consistently.

Three areas of knowledge are essential for salespeople today:

1. *Comprehensive knowledge of the customer's industry, company, and strategies.* Salespeople in all world markets today are expected to be familiar with the customer's industry and the impact of new global competitors. Corporate Websites and industry news groups make it easier than ever for salespeople to stay on top of customer organization and marketplace evolution. But the availability of information does not translate into competitive advantage unless a salesperson can apply what he or she knows to the direct benefit of the customer. Particu-larly in North America, salespeople are also expected to pro-vide insight into how their product can support the corporate strategies their customers deploy, from implementing total

quality to reducing the supplier base. As a customer of Scott Paper Company (United States) described it, he values salespeople who focus not just on their needs but also on those of their customers—i.e., on the customer's customer. "What's unique about Scott's salespeople is that we work in partnership with them to reach the end user. They always keep in mind that the ultimate customer is the end user. This is different from most of their competitors, who think of the distributor as the ultimate customer."

2. *In-depth knowledge of their own company's full range of product and service applications . . . and the products and services their competition offers.* The freewheeling information economy facilitated by the Internet has produced greater "information expectations" from customers. As a salesperson for Scott Paper Company (United States) noted, "Customers don't have time to become experts in what I sell, so they rely on me to have the expertise." Customers base their decisions not only on how well a product meets their needs but also on how all the related services that supplier organizations offer can support their strategy and help them compete.[2] Customers expect the salesperson's expertise to extend to competitive products as well. According to a salesperson from Ordo (France), "Customers don't want to work with salespeople who know only their own products. Salespeople also have to know the products and services offered by competitors." This challenge gets greater every day, as product life cycles contract and innovation advantage can be measured in months or even weeks. Some customers expect even more. A customer of Rank Xerox in Sweden, for example, singled out that company's salespeople because they were "better at cooperating with other suppliers to find the complete solution." Hewlett-Packard (United States) has told its salespeople that they must not only be knowledgeable about their own products but also complementary products from its many partners. Like other organizations truly focused on the customer, Hewlett-Packard (HP) goes the extra distance to focus on the customer's total needs; for example, HP will wrap the customer's non-HP equipment in the service blanket that covers HP products.

---

[2]For their part, salespeople view this expanded demand as an opportunity to practice some healthy protectionism. As a salesperson at Scott Paper Company put it, "We look at an account on the basis of the services we can offer to protect our position."

3. *A thorough understanding of general business management.* Customers expect the salespeople they work with to have the critical business judgment and expertise necessary to *use* the strategic information given them. Said a customer of Scott Paper Company (United States), "A good salesperson can answer the question, 'If we decide to do business with you, how will our business grow?' I always ask salespeople this question, but I rarely get an answer." As a salesperson from Rank Xerox (The Netherlands) put it, "A client expects you to think with him about his business, his alternatives, and what the return would be for each alternative chosen." In some customer organizations, this expectation may have grown out of the decision to use fewer suppliers (a growing trend), which creates the need for a greater sense of partnership, or trust, between customers and the limited number of suppliers they engage.

In addition, customers say that one of the most significant factors influencing the supplier's ability to meet their expectations is the tenure of the salesperson in the sales assignment. Customers put a high value on working with salespeople who know the customer's organization intimately. Further, they resent the time required to orient a supplier's new salesperson to their business.[3]

Xerox Corporation (United States) recognizes this critical need and has developed a program to assign senior managers to selected accounts, with the specific goal of providing continuity and a consistent presence for the customer. Of course, this approach has many other benefits as well, not the least of which is what senior managers learn as a result of having direct customer contact.

Other sales organizations are unable to stem the turnover tide in the current period of robust opportunity. Those companies have opted to use technology to ensure continuity for customers and a leg up for new salespeople. By making sure that salespeople build solid account history data into a Customer Resource Management (CRM) tool, companies can save their customers, and new account reps, from the laborious task of building relationships from scratch. After all, from the customer's point of view, if you are starting over with an established vendor, why not survey and level the playing field of

---

[3]Importantly, customers of the companies in our research frequently volunteered this point, yet few of the sales organizations brought it up.

possible solution providers? For the sales organization, that can mean that a relationship that may have been secure becomes unraveled. So, for sales force turnover to have reduced impact on sales effectiveness, CRM-driven continuity in the customer-supplier relationship is a big advantage.

So, what is the reward for equipping salespeople with high levels of knowledge and business savvy—and the skill needed to apply them? Customers tend to view salespeople who meet their expectations as a *resource*—as people who can help them meet their goals, educate and inform them, solve business problems over the long term, and meet the needs of their internal and external customers. In short, the reward is customer *loyalty*. As a customer of Ordo (France) put it, "The more competent the salespeople are, the more I rely on that company."

THE EVOLUTION
IN PROFESSIONAL RELATIONSHIPS

"Golf games and friendships don't guarantee customer loyalty anymore. It's the performance that counts."

—Salesperson, Scott Paper Company
(United States)

Strong customer relationships are built on rapport, trust, and respect between the salesperson and the customer. In the past, many salespeople focused on developing these qualities on a personal level as a way to differentiate themselves. This was a successful and accepted strategy. As a sales manager from Union Pacific Railroad (United States) put it, "Before deregulation, when most prices were the same, selling was a matter of building a social relationship. You took customers out to lunch or dinner, and, if they liked you, you got the business."

Today, developing business through social skills is still important, but it's not enough. Its success depends too much on the compatibility of the personalities involved. If a salesperson should accept another position or, for whatever reason, relinquish control of the account, the sales organization is highly vulnerable to losing the business entirely. This state of affairs would reach its lowest point when the salesperson moved to a competitor and, primarily because of the social bond, took customers with him.

Furthermore, customers can no longer rationalize the choice between two suppliers on the basis of friendship. They must justify the choice on the basis of *business* factors. For example, a study of buyers in the electric utility industry found that credibility, reliability, and responsiveness were the most highly rated salesperson competencies and that "degree of initiative taken" was considered more important than friendship in making a sale.[4]

Certainly rapport, trust, and respect on a personal level are still important. But today, business relationships are based less on personal small talk and more on the salesperson's ability to address the customer's business concerns. Trust comes less through the salesperson's persuasiveness and charm and more from his or her ability to substantiate—through actual performance—the truth of his or her claims.

THE ULTIMATE CHALLENGE: DEFINING A SALES STRATEGY

"The keys to success will be increased productivity of our sales force, measurement of the sales process, feedback from customers that drives continuous process improvement, and identification of alternate distribution channels for different segments of our business."

—Vice president, Hewlett-Packard Company
(United States)

Many leading sales organizations have defined a sales strategy that will differentiate them through the strength of their salespeople's business performance with customers. They believe this strategy will give them a sustainable, competitively distinct advantage in a demanding, unpredictable business environment.

The sales leaders that AchieveGlobal studied are focused on the one thing they have a great deal of control over and that their competition will find most difficult to copy—that is, the quality and durability of the relationship between their organization and their customers. This is true at both the micro level (salesperson-to-customer contact) and the macro level (organization to organization).

---

[4]Hayes and S. W. Harley, "How Buyers View Industrial Salespeople," *Industrial Marketing Management* 18 (1989), pp. 73–80.

Northwestern Mutual Life Insurance Company:
"Sociable Professionalism"

Northwestern Mutual Life Insurance Company's (United States) approach to building trust and rapport with customers is a reflection of the transition from social to professional business relationships.

During their sales calls to prospective customers, Northwestern Mutual's agents use a survey form called the FactFinder, which contains questions about a client's assets, liabilities, monthly expenses, investments, insurance coverage, and other financial details.

Agents work with the customers to complete the form in a conversational style using questioning skills and listening skills. The agent also responds empathetically to the personal information shared. This approach is designed to accomplish two objectives: to identify the client's needs and to build the relationship. By the time the FactFinder is completed, a sense of trust and rapport has been created and the foundation for a solid business relationship is built.

These organizations are working to establish an *ideal business relationship* with every customer with whom they choose to do business.

Each of them is using a different array of concepts, practices, and tactics to achieve this goal: team selling, sales force automation/customer resource management, reengineering, sales-focused quality management efforts, and continuous improvement are among them. As you will read in the following chapters, some are familiar approaches, but these organizations have applied them with a unique structure, discipline, or focus. In any case, all of these leading organizations are committed to flawlessly executing their strategies, because they've learned that the success of any strategy is determined largely by the quality of its execution.

Managing, tracking, and improving all the factors by which the sales organization develops customer relationships is a daunting task. One AchieveGlobal study showed that for a sales force to achieve its goals for both customer satisfaction and profitability, sales management may need to monitor at least 45 separate activi-

---

Ideal Business Relationship:

A business relationship characterized by a sense of rapport, trust, and respect between the salesperson and customer, with the expectation that their organizations will do business over the long term and in a mutually beneficial way.

---

ties ranging from "ensuring that sales managers regularly coach and give feedback to salespeople" to "forecasting sales accurately."[5]

To bring order and priority to the task, several of the leading sales organizations that AchieveGlobal studied are applying the principles of business process management to their business relationship-building efforts. Their pioneering work, described in the following chapter, will set a new standard for sales excellence and performance.

BEST PRACTICES AND GUIDING PRINCIPLES

Ensure that your customer satisfaction measurement system assesses what customers in three major world markets said was most important:

- Salespeople who are honest; salespeople who keep promises.
- Products and services that are delivered on time, perform as anticipated, and are consistent in quality.
- A supplier organization that can be trusted.

Ensure that the people in your sales organization have a common understanding and share a common vision in the following areas. Ask yourself:

1. What are the dynamics of our market?
- What is our customer profile?
- How are our customers changing?

---

[5]AchieveGlobal, *Sales Productivity Action Planning Guide* (1992).

- What are our customers' expectations of our sales force? How are these expectations changing?
- What is influencing those changes?
- How are our competitors changing?

2. What is our sales strategy?

- How will our sales strategy help us to differentiate our company from the competition? Build profits and stay competitive? Improve customer satisfaction?
- What are our competitors' sales strategies?

3. How does our sales organization add value?

- What value does our sales force add for our customers, beyond what our products or services provide? What value *could* they add?
- How do our competitors' sales forces add value for their customers?

4. What are our sales priorities?

- What priority do our salespeople give these three goals: revenue, profits, customer satisfaction?
- What priority do our sales managers give them?
- What priority does our compensation plan give to those three goals, and is it aligned with our sales priorities?

II

BUILDING CUSTOMER RELATIONSHIPS

*"A good salesperson can answer this question for every customer:
'If we decide to work together, how will the customer's business
grow?' "*

Chapter Three

Focusing the Organization Outward

"You're in it together, your interests are the same."

—Customer, Scott Paper Company
(United States)

- The importance of vision
- Defining a value proposition
- Aligning the entire organization with the vision
- Preparing the entire organization to sell

At one time, a company could satisfy a customer solely by producing a reliable product. In today's highly competitive environment, that's no longer the case, since high product quality and performance are becoming the norm at the world's most progressive companies. Informed consumers can buy from a myriad of sources.

So what does it take for the entire organization to succeed? Our research and experience with the world's leading sales organizations indicates that a strong customer focus is the key to a company's continued growth and expansion. Successful global organizations are creating new strategies that are based on the needs and expectations of their customers.

For proof, just look at the corporate mission statements of any of today's leading companies. IBM's reads: "We translate advanced technologies into *value for our customers* as the world's largest information services company. Our professionals worldwide provide expertise within specific industries, consulting services, systems integration and solution development and technical support."

Similarly, one of Hewlett-Packard's corporate objectives reads: "To provide products and services of the highest quality and the greatest possible *value to our customers,* thereby gaining and holding their respect and loyalty." And Xerox Corporation follows six core *values:*

- We succeed through satisfied customers.
- We aspire to deliver quality and excellence in all that we do.
- We require premium return on assets.
- We use technology to deliver market leadership.
- We value our employees.
- We behave responsibly as a corporate citizen.

As you may have noticed, the word *value* appears repeatedly in these statements. High-performance organizations are looking outward, identifying the value customers get from their products and services—and then incorporating what they learn into developing new customer-centered visions and sales strategies that meet these changing demands.

Customer-driven corporations are also recognizing that not only their sales organizations must understand and communicate this value message to customers. Rather, high-performing sales organizations are those where the entire company is consciously involved in selling itself to the customer. It requires the commitment and participation of every person in the organization, regardless of function. The belief throughout the company that "everybody sells" is essential to success.

In this chapter, we will explore how vision can unify the organization around similar goals and motivate everyone to work toward building long-lasting, mutually beneficial business relationships with customers.

ESTABLISHING A VISION

Too often, a vision statement is viewed as just words on paper, to be displayed on marketing and promotional material but having no further meaning for a company or its employees. An effective vision is anything but that.

Unlike a mission statement, which is usually a broader, more conceptual statement of an organization's operating philosophy, a vision serves as a unifying and motivating *objective* for the entire or-

---

Vision

An organization's statement of where in the marketplace it hopes to be at a certain point in the future.

---

ganization. Strategies are developed and tested against the vision. All decisions are made in light of how they will bring the organization closer to its vision.

A Louis Harris and Associates study sponsored by Achieve Global found that the most effective corporate visions illustrate *clarity of focus* and *collective understanding.*

Clarity of Focus: Visions should be stated clearly and succinctly. Effective visions also have a clear and unequivocal focus. In the Harris and Associates study, most vision statements fell into one of three general categories:

1. Improve growth through diversification (31 percent)
2. Increase domestic market share (27 percent)
3. Become a leader in the industry or business (21 percent)

Collective Understanding: To avoid the words-on-paper syndrome that makes a clearly defined vision useless, executives at top-performing companies make sure that the vision is communicated to and understood by everyone throughout the organization. This collective understanding ensures that every employee knows:

1. The organization's goals and directions
2. Priorities in terms of customers as well as product and service offerings
3. What differentiates their organization from others

Hewlett-Packard exemplifies a company that continually strives for collective understanding of its vision. Every person we interviewed at this organization expressed a clear understanding of the company's competitive issues, goals, and key strategies. Most strikingly, three levels of sales managers, several sales representatives, and the vice president of sales all described the sales strategy using similar words and phrases.

This collective understanding is even expressed in Hewlett-Packard's own statement of corporate objectives:

"HP's view of its relationships with customers has been shaped by two basic beliefs. First, we believe the reason HP exists is to satisfy real customer needs. Second, we believe those needs can be fully satisfied *only with the active participation and dedication of everyone in the company.* We must listen attentively to our customers to understand and respond to their current needs and to anticipate their future needs."

COMMIT TO A CUSTOMER FOCUS

"The top guys know everything there is to know about their customers."

—Customer, Océ (The Netherlands)

To develop a customer-driven vision statement and the strategies and tactics to support that vision, organizations must analyze their markets, as well as the needs of their current and prospective customers. Studies on buyer-seller relationships reveal why an organizational commitment to customer focus translates into customer loyalty. As part of our *Profiles in Customer Loyalty* research, we asked buyers in different industries around the world what aspects of a supplier organization contributed most to their continued overall satisfaction with that supplier. Six factors emerged:

1. *Business expertise and image*—the organization's business stability, name recognition, and industry leadership.
2. *Dedication to customer*—the perceived credibility of the organization and the ability of the staff to solve business problems and function as a long-term business partner.
3. *Account sensitivity and guidance*—the organization's market sensitivity and responsiveness to issues related to price, punctuality, and quality standards.
4. *Product performance and quality*—how well the product or service actually performs.
5. *Service department excellence*—the interpersonal skills, reliability, and competence of customer service personnel.
6. *Confirmations of capabilities*—proof of product or service claims.

Note that the whole organization is represented by these factors—from production to distribution to accounts receivable. Again, everyone in the company must be focused on the customer, regardless of his or her function.

Having a customer-centered focus influences many of the strategic decisions that must be made in order to realize the organization's vision. For example:

1. Segmenting your customers—deciding to whom you want to sell and if how and what you sell and service should be different for different groups of customers.
2. Opening new business within desired organizations.
3. Deploying the sales force in the most effective manner (e.g., geographic, key account, telemarketing).
4. Choosing the right distribution channels.
5. Setting appropriate sales and service goals.
6. Scanning the market—keeping an eye on the competition as well as looking for new product and service opportunities.

In the following section, we will discuss one of these strategic decisions, segmentation, in greater depth.

DEFINE CUSTOMER VALUES

"They respond to special requests to serve the customer."

—Customer, American Airlines

Identifying the value that customers realize from working with an organization and its products and services is a useful step in developing a customer-driven vision. Sometimes called a *value proposition*, organizations articulate what their customers will get from doing business with them. The value statement of companies can easily be seen in the home pages of many Websites. For example, The Quaker Oats Company's value statement (which they call *The Mission*) reads: "To meet the needs of consumers through innovative marketing and manufacturing of healthful, good-tasting products *that contribute to a healthy lifestyle and consumer well-being* around the world, yielding above-average returns over time for our shareholders."

And part of Kimberly-Clark's "Who We Are" statement reads: "Superior Performance: At Kimberly-Clark, we believe in creating superior products which best meet consumers' and customers' needs. We believe in *developing brands that are truly meaningful to people* and are respected around the world. We strive to be one of the world's most successful companies, dedicated to winning through hard work and fair play."

How do organizations establish the customer's values? This grows out of gathering information from the market and from the organization's customers through such mechanisms as market research, segmentation studies, win/loss programs, customer loyalty studies, and feedback from salespeople. Now that technology is broadening the ways to acquire information, you can also add the use of e-mail information and Internet learning to the list.

Through research, you will be able to develop a strategy that best serves your customers, or *groups of common customers.* Increasingly, companies are finding that it is better to segment customers by customer needs and types, rather than by a product-focused regional structure. Salespeople at 3M, for example, are serving vertical industries (such as automotive, general industrial, and government) to focus on common needs and solutions. *Reason:* When a salesperson has to cover an entire territory with a wide range of customer industries and conflicting needs, he or she often has to take a "one size fits all" approach. This waters down the service provided, which limits customer value and diminishes the strength of the relationship. With segmentation, you can use a similar sales model to best reach each customer segment's needs. The salesperson can more easily build and maintain long-term customer associations, which are vital in this competitive marketplace.

Segmentation also allows an organization to examine how best to serve customers with varying levels of needs. For example, some customers may require a dedicated salesperson to help discuss and problem-solve the complexity of products and services they need as well as any special ongoing requirements; while other customers, who have less complicated situations, can be served more efficiently by a telemarketing unit.

Many organizations' immediate customer is not the end user, but rather a distributor, purchasing agent, or retailer. So while building value with your immediate customer, it's also important to establish, where appropriate, value with end users—your customer's customers.

As a customer said about Scott Paper: "What's unique about Scott is that they don't think about the distributor as being the ultimate customer. We work in partnership with them, to reach the end user. They always keep in mind that the end user is the ultimate customer. This is different from most of their competitors who think of the distributor as the ultimate customer. They really understand the idea of partnership, and they really believe it."

Along with value, it is also important to create customer *loyalty* with the end user. NEC Corporation, for example, provided rebates to end users of their award-winning PC laser printers. Even though NEC is a well-known brand and their PCs are priced competitively, the company realized the value of creating customer loyalty with the end user. Consumers who buy on quality may purchase NEC anyway. However, the rebate offer may get more of those customers who purchase on price alone to try NEC products and become loyal buyers. Organizations can engender loyalty by providing special services or perks to their best customers. Witness the incredible popularity of frequent-flyer programs and hotel frequent-stay programs. Virtually all airlines and global hotel chains keep a database of their customers' individual preferences. Such organizations understand the saying, "A satisfied customer will tell five people about an experience, while each dissatisfied customer will tell nine."

DEVELOP A STRATEGIC FOCUS

"They (salespeople) need the typical traits, such as working hard, high energy level, but the vision—the ability to see the customer's unique requirements and the best fit—is the thing that separates the best performers."

—Vice President, Xerox

To realize their visions, organizations implement a wide range of initiatives, such as quality systems, cost controls, sales force automation, reengineering, and continuous improvement. These initiatives are as varied as the organizations themselves. But to effectively reach its vision, an organization must make sure that every initiative has the proper strategic focus.

Strategic focus refers to the guiding principle behind all initiatives undertaken by an organization to achieve its vision. The only appropriate strategic focus of any initiative to improve sales performance is on *strengthening the quality and durability of the relationship between an organization and its customers and potential customers.* Once again, it's critical that everyone in the company understands how a strategic focus helps bring the organization closer to achieving its vision. This means that all employees have to be willful (committed, not merely compliant) and skillful (possessing the necessary knowledge, skills, and attitudes) to put the strategy into action.

The Grainger Industrial Supply division of W. W. Grainger has a strategic focus on solving customer problems. They ensure that not only salespeople but everyone throughout the organization focus on the customer and find solutions to their problems. Their concept of the "enterprise sales force" ensures that product managers, marketing representatives, and anyone involved in providing information that will be used by the sales force keep in mind the customer.

"Anyone who gets in front of the sales force with information has to be prepared to talk about and educate them about the condition or problem that might exist within the customer organization that can be solved with our products," says Brian Spanswick of Grainger's Workforce Productivity Improvement Group. "It's not enough to just focus on product features. Our sales force needs to be able to demonstrate real value to our customers. It's up to everyone in the company to help them do that."

Some of the behaviors that top-performing organizations have demonstrated to ensure that this customer-driven strategic focus is integrated throughout the organization include:

1. Hiring the best available candidates and clearly communicating job performance expectations as they relate to the strategic focus.
2. Training and coaching employees to understand and meet or exceed customer expectations.
3. Giving employees the resources, support, and authority to serve customers effectively.
4. Motivating employees to focus on customer-driven service through incentive and recognition programs.

CREATE AN EMPOWERED ENVIRONMENT

"The organization must allow decision making and accountability to be passed down the line. There has to be a culture that trusts people to make the right decisions, and accepts that mistakes will be made when new ideas are tried."

—Vice president, Allen & Hanbury

We noted earlier that even the best vision statement is meaningless, regardless of how well it states customer values, unless everyone in the organization lives and breathes it.

Through our research, AchieveGlobal has found that the strategies derived from this vision will only work in a supportive cultural environment. In these empowered cultures, the organization is committed to ensuring that people at all levels feel motivated and authorized to make decisions that support the strategy and vision. Cultural empowerment within an organization is characterized by the following:

1. *Management leads by example.* Top managers are not only committed to living what they preach, they actually do live what they preach.

2. *Information flows freely.* Individuals are encouraged to share their knowledge and expertise with others. Mechanisms are in place so that information crosses organizational boundaries smoothly, with minimal bureaucratic static.

3. *Continuous learning and professional development are encouraged.* Top management encourages and enables all employees to learn. Acquiring new skills is rewarded; failures are examined for valuable improvement lessons—not for assigning blame.

4. *Trust is pervasive.* Dissension and challenge in the name of improvement are encouraged. Employees are valued for their ideas and diverse thinking.

5. *Risk-taking is encouraged.* Creativity is considered necessary for success.

6. *Feedback is welcome.* Feedback is viewed as essential to maintaining the correct focus on, and progress toward, the organization's vision.

In this type of supportive environment, there is a free and open exchange of information among functions. This, most importantly, includes a sharing of customer information, such as customer needs, buying habits, purchases, complaints, and compliments. Units in an organization can capitalize on this information exchange to further strengthen customer loyalty. For example, Hewlett-Packard distributes a newsletter, "HP-At-Home," to customers of different business units. This builds customer loyalty for the whole HP organization, rather than for just one service or product line.

CONCLUSION

An increasing number of companies realize that if they don't meet customer expectations—regardless of the amount of resources expended—they'll have fewer customers to serve and much less loyalty from those who remain as buyers. Not only are customers increasing their demands, but they are also becoming more knowledgeable and discriminating; they only continue going to those companies that provide value-added services and products.

This means that any advantage a company gains through a new or innovative product or service is temporary at best. Instead, an organization must look for other ways to build loyal customer partnerships.

As a result, leading industry organizations are finding it essential to create a customer-driven vision and strategy. In addition, they understand that this vision must be disseminated companywide. They must get the support and buy-in of every employee and create an empowered environment where information about the customer flows readily across functional boundaries. This ensures that a vision statement becomes much more than words written by executives that appear on a Website or product packaging solely for marketing purposes. Instead, the vision becomes a viable part of every employee's words and actions, assuring that each interaction with a customer embodies the values that customer has come to expect from this organization.

BEST PRACTICES AND GUIDING PRINCIPLES

To remain competitive, top-performing organizations must

- Look outward and develop a customer-driven focus.
- View its mission as a meaningful, working model that describes what that organization strives to accomplish in the future.
- Define a vision and strategic focus by measuring customer values and expectations either through traditional methods such as surveys and interviews or new technology such as e-mail or the Internet.
- Communicate a companywide vision so that each employee's actions clearly illustrate what that vision is to achieve.
- Create a culture that supports the flow of information across departments and functions, the continuous learning of all employees, and the input from people at every level of the organization.

Chapter Four

The Customer Relationship Process: Creating Loyal Partners

"For continuous process improvement, you have to have in place a model and all the measures and tools to know how you are performing at any moment. Then you have to keep pushing the model to get more productivity out of it, to get higher quality from the sales process, and to get more customer satisfaction at the other end. You may be very comfortable with your model, and it may even be a breakthrough. But others will be watching you and seeking ways to improve it. You cannot rest on your laurels."

—Vice president, Hewlett-Packard Company
(United States)

- How do sales organizations "reengineer"?
- What is a Customer Relationship Process? What does it look like? How can it help your company become more competitive?
- What is the role of salespeople in insuring the success of the Customer Relationship Process?
- What is the value of mapping the process?

As we discussed in previous chapters, today's leading sales organizations are determined to differentiate themselves through the strength of their relationships with their customers. As the CEO of Alexander Howden NA states: "Anybody can copy a product, anyone can copy a service level, but if you have a unique relationship, this is much more difficult to copy, thus maintaining your competitive advantage."

More and more organizations have found that documenting their ideal customer relationship is one of the strategic tools that can help them achieve their growth, loyalty, and profitability goals. They create a *map* to help them focus on the activities that truly make a difference to customers—and to avoid wasting resources and time on misdirected efforts. The map directly applies process engineering, measurement, and continuous improvement ideas to the competitive, hard-to-differentiate sales environment of today.

These organizations—including Xerox Corporation, Scott Paper Company, and Hewlett-Packard Company in North America; AMP in Singapore, Sweden, Norway, and the United States; Canadian Liquid Air; Alexander Howden NA; and Avis Fleet Services in Europe—define and communicate their priorities to their salespeople and their customers. They reengineer and restructure to better meet customers' needs and formulate and execute powerful, competitively distinct strategies for building stronger customer relationships.

Though these ideas are logical and simple, they are sometimes revolutionary for a sales organization—a functional area that has long been characterized by entrepreneurial spirit, fierce individualism, and an aversion to detailed analysis and measurement. Yet, they are producing powerful answers to the fundamental question that plagues every top sales executive: how to improve both sales performance and customer satisfaction—profitably.

Alexander Howden NA (AHNA) for example, has begun receiving calls from customers for help with things it has never helped with in the past. This new business has developed because the customers appreciate AHNA's focus on them—a focus that the map helped AHNA accomplish. This chapter looks at how some organizations are putting this simple but elegant strategy into practice.

BEYOND TOTAL QUALITY TO CUSTOMER LOYALTY

"The quality initiative focused us on satisfying a customer's total requirements."

—Vice president, Xerox Corporation
(United States)

Total quality management (TQM)—whose principles, processes, and rigorous methods were the buzzwords of the previous decade and once confined to the manufacturing plant—found their way into almost every functional area in organization and industries of every description. Its leaders (W. Edwards Deming, Joseph M. Juran, Philip Crosby, David Garvin, Armand Feigenbaum, and Genichi Taguchi, to name some of the most prominent) schooled an entire generation in quality principles.

While the TQM furor has cooled down substantially, the fundamental principles have had a tremendous impact on forward-thinking sales organizations. The idea of process reengineering, measurement, and the like through mapping has produced extraordinary results. This approach defines quality in terms of customers' needs, recognizes the tie between quality and profitability, includes quality planning in the strategic planning process, and stresses continuous organization-wide improvement.

Typically, the goal of quality management was to analyze, streamline, and perfect the organization's business processes so that the organization can meet or exceed customers' expectations at the least cost. That goal is still valid, and its ideas have contributed to the pursuit of customer loyalty.

Companies throughout the industrialized world embraced total quality management—with good reason. "We found that businesses labeled 'high quality' by their customers are two to three times more profitable than businesses ranked lowest on the quality scale," observed Devereaux Dion, senior vice president of the Strategic Planning Institute (SPI), a Cambridge, Massachusetts not-for-profit research organization.[1] SPI bases its conclusion on cumulative data from its Profit Impact of Market Strategy (PIMS) database, which includes financial, marketing, and competitive information on 3000 participating business units.

Customer loyalty, as we see clearly today, is highly profitable because it is less costly to retain satisfied, loyal customers than it is to gain new ones.

It is easiest for supplier organizations to view and analyze their business processes from their own vantage point. "The challenge is, looking internally to get new business won't work, especially if you are selling commodities, which most of the world is. You need to look to your customers—what their strategies are and how they

---

[1]Frederick F. Reichheld, *The Loyalty Effect* (Boston: Harvard Business School Press , 1996).

want to be perceived in the marketplace. With this you can build a relationship and in turn improve the flow of business," says the CEO of Alexander Howden NA.

To gain a clear understanding of the activities that influence customer loyalty, it is critical to examine business processes from the customer's point of view. For example, sales organizations have traditionally defined their activities as a sales cycle. With a shift in emphasis on customers, some organizations have instead begun to focus on the Customer Relationship Process (CRP).

The Customer Relationship Process is literally what the *customer* experiences when interacting with a supplier organization's people. It consists of the entire sequence of person-to-person business encounters—from the sales organization to any functional area—that comprise the customer's full experience with the supplier organization. Most of these encounters occur with the organization's front-line sales and service professionals. In fact, some organizations define their Customer Relationship Process as the combination of the sales cycle (sales performance process) and the service cycle—the activities that can further cement the relationship and customer loyalty, leading to a true partnership.

What is immediately apparent is that every business, from the one-person shop to the multibillion-dollar corporation, has a process for working with customers, that is, a Customer Relationship Process. Most organizations, however, have never defined it or analyzed it; and because they don't isolate it and critique it, they cannot manage it or improve it.

Some organizations, however, are using good "old-fashioned" quality principles and tools to define, study, and document their CRP. Whether they choose to map the process using flowcharting or to describe it in detailed text, their goal is to identify the activities that will help them close the gap between customer expectations and what their organization delivers. Documenting the CRP helps

---

Customer Relationship Process

The sequence of activities performed by the people who are in direct contact with customers that enable the supplier organization to meet or exceed customer requirements and ensure customer loyalty.

these organizations uncover vast amounts of critical information that they can use to make strategically important decisions about their organization's direction, processes and procedures, hiring practices, training and coaching priorities, and rewards systems (Figure 4-1.) Mapping its CRP will help an organization to:

- Identify and analyze its people's interactions with customers.
- Measure its people's performance against customer requirements and competitors' performance.
- Involve customers in a dialogue about how the organization can change its CRP to better meet their needs.
- Establish a common language that can be used within the organization and with customers to describe how the organization works with customers now—and how it would like to work with them in the future.
- Clarify the roles, high-value activities, and competencies required of the front-line people whose daily interactions build the customer relationship.
- Standardize and replicate the actions and behaviors that customers most value and that can differentiate the organization from its competition.
- Better understand—and meet—the needs of various market segments by examining the CRPs that best meet their needs.
- Help organizations deliver on their promise to customers.
- Reduce uncertainty in the relationship with customers.
- Understand the whole process of interaction with the customer, so that organization can improve upon it and keep a competitive advantage.

As Michael Porter wrote in *The Competitive Advantage of Nations*, "Competitive advantage grows out of the way firms organize and perform discrete activities. . . Firms create value for their buyers through performing these activities. To gain competitive advantage over its rivals, a firm must either provide comparable buyer value but perform activities more efficiently than its competitors (lower cost), or perform activities in a unique way that creates greater buyer value and commands a premium price (differentiation)."[2]

---

[2]Michael Porter, *The Competitive Advantage of Nations* (New York: The Free Press, 1990), p. 40.

FIGURE 4–1
The Performance Model

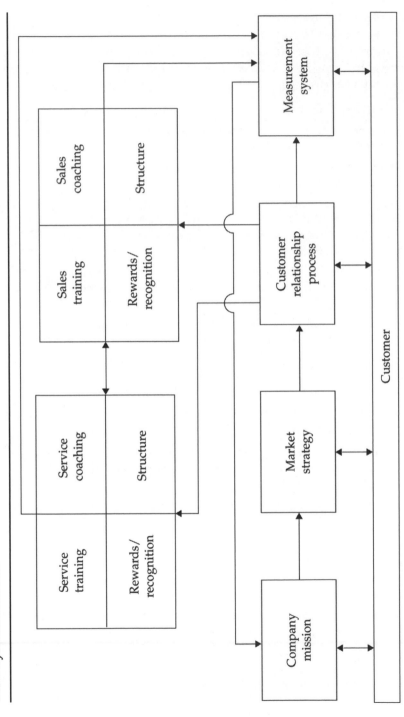

Mapping, analyzing, and improving the critical activities of the CRP cannot eliminate all the variables (e.g., a competitor's actions or a key contact moving on to a new job). However, following these steps can enable the supplier organization to improve the quality, speed, and accuracy of the actions it *can* control. It can help an organization identify activities that are critical, eliminate unnecessary activities, and thereby provide a method to control or reduce the costs associated with sales and service.

Frederick F. Reichheld, in *The Loyalty Effect* says that "Consistently high retention (of customers) can create tremendous competitive advantage, boost employee morale, produce unexpected bonuses in productivity and growth, even reduce the cost of capital."[3] Continually improving the CRP increases the chances that every interaction with customers will improve the business relationship and ultimately create customer loyalty.

FOCUSING ON CRITICAL ACTIVITIES

"We have always measured sales performance in terms of end results—in terms of quota, growth, and new accounts. That may not be the best way to measure performance. We also need to look at the steps of the process and measure those. If we do well at the steps, the end results will absolutely come."

—Sales manager, Hewlett-Packard Company
(United States)

Organizations that are using the CRP as a framework offer this advice: The key to achieving cost-effective delivery of services is to focus on the few activities that are most critical to productivity and customer loyalty. These are high-leverage activities that an organization must perform correctly to satisfy customers, and the ones that differentiate it from competition.

Typically, these organizations develop a user-friendly flowchart or description that condenses the complex picture of how the organization builds relationships into a handful of phases and their associated activities.

---

[3]Frederick F. Reichheld, *The Loyalty Effect* (Boston: Harvard Business School Press, , 1996).

Most CRP-map documents start out as text that lists the phases and their activities. The example shown in the following box is of one organization's Customer Relationship Process.

Customer Relationship Process—Company X

Phase 1: Establish the relationship.

- Qualify the prospect.
- Gather information.
- Introduce capabilities.

Phase 2: Analyze the customer's requirements.

- Define the requirements.
- Clarify the buying process.
- Validate requirements.

Phase 3: Recommend solutions and gain commitment.

- Validate proposal with customer.
- Prepare a presentation.
- Gain commitment to specific recommendations.

Phase 4: Implement the recommendations.

- Initiate setup.
- Monitor installation.
- Initiate follow-up.

Phase 5: Maintain and expand the business relationship.

- Institute follow-up procedures.
- Initiate formal review of customer satisfaction.
- Identify new opportunities.

The same CRP, "mapped" as a flowchart (see Figure 4-2) portrays a snapshot of the process. The level of detail with which an organization describes its CRP phases and activities depends largely on the organization's culture, the complexity of its products and services, and the intensity and nature of its competitive challenges. However, "keep it simple" is the advice of most of the pioneers who are currently using it.

FIGURE 4–2
Customer Relationship Process

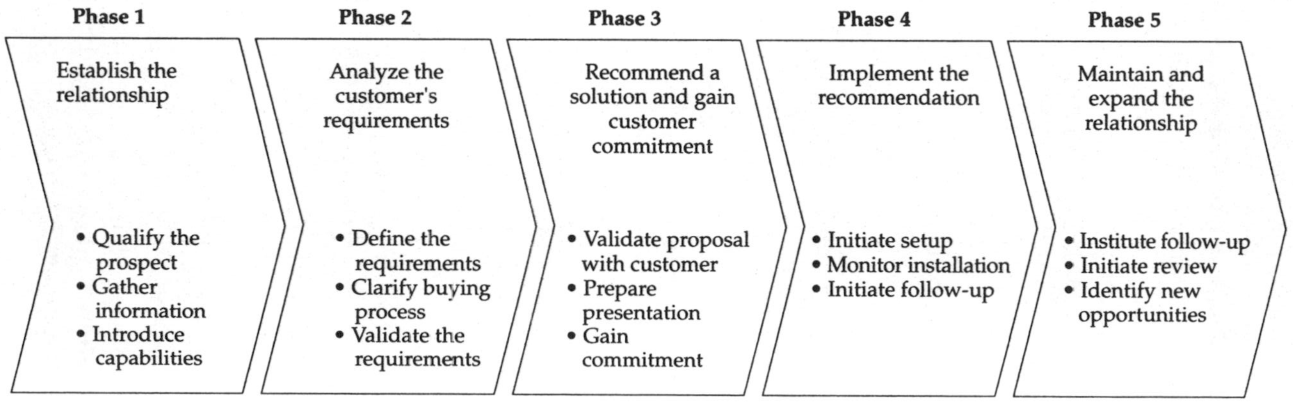

Phase 1	Phase 2	Phase 3	Phase 4	Phase 5
Establish the relationship	Analyze the customer's requirements	Recommend a solution and gain customer commitment	Implement the recommendation	Maintain and expand the relationship
• Qualify the prospect • Gather information • Introduce capabilities	• Define the requirements • Clarify buying process • Validate the requirements	• Validate proposal with customer • Prepare presentation • Gain commitment	• Initiate setup • Monitor installation • Initiate follow-up	• Institute follow-up • Initiate review • Identify new opportunities

The interactions between salespeople and customers figure prominently in a CRP; the data about these interactions can be used to evaluate a sales strategy and often, when done in isolation, are referred to as a "Sales Performance Process Map. (SPPM)" A full CRP, however, focuses on the interactions with everyone who touches the customer, with sales often being the most critical. Other organizations use the CRP framework to examine their customers' experiences with the supplier organization's service people or to develop a marketing strategy. The following section looks at how two organizations, AMP Nordic and Premier Hospital Supply, Inc.,[4] have used CRP mapping to develop and communicate strategies in two critical areas: sales and marketing.

APPLYING CRP MAPPING TO IMPROVE COMPETITIVENESS: TWO CASE STUDIES

AMP Nordic

AMP Nordic manufactures, markets, and sells electronic and electrical connectors to the telecom, automotive, and industrial manufacturing sector. Over the past 5 years, AMP has worked diligently to achieve quality throughout the organization by achieving Nordic ISO 9000 certification, and working with MRP2 and VAM. The missing link between all of AMP's quality efforts and the marketplace? The Customer Relationship Process. AMP sees the value of CRP as a way to fit all of the jigsaw pieces together to show the market its complete quality program.

The process AMP used to develop the CRP was highly customer focused. During the development of the map, AMP worked with purchasing and development managers representing its most important customers. These customers participated in identifying the phases of the CRP, the definitions and of course, identifying of customer expectations (see Table 4-1).

Although AMP only recently developed their CRP (1998–99), the process has already received extremely positive reactions: "No one in the industry had shown any knowledge or concern about this process before," stated one key customer.

---

[4]Not this organization's real name.

TABLE 4-1
Customer Relationship Process with Customer Expectations—
AMP Nordic

1. Earn the right.
   • Pick up signals and react when needed.
   • Show commitment and react quickly.
   • Focus on actual situation.
2. Establish contacts.
   • Follow agreed ways to interact.
   • By interacting with the right contacts, build a thorough under-
     standing of our organization and its functions.
   • Define needs and demands.
   • Continuously clarify and confirm to obtain a common
     estimation/understanding of our and our customers' needs.
3. Define solutions.
   • Have one person coordinating AMP's efforts.
   • As a supplier, have full insight into relevant rules and standards.
4. Draw up agreements.
   • Quickly inform the customer of any deviation from proposed
     agreement.
   • Give suggestions for solution if deviations from the proposed
     agreement occur.
5. Follow up.
   • Measure and follow up on agreed targets.
   • Reach agreed targets.
6. Develop.
   • AMP should be in the front line both technically and commercially.
   • Be flexible and sensitive to customer needs.
   • Show a high level of ambition.

Applications for the CRP are many—AMP uses it as a "letter of
intent" with customers, as an internal policy document for all employees, and as a tool for demonstrating to its marketplace the value
it brings to the customer-supplier relationship.

The payoff of the CRP for AMP is already evident—a big piece of
business was gained against heavy competition, because the customer could see clearly from their efforts that AMP was a supplier
to trust.

Premier Hospital Supply, Inc.

Another example of a company that has used CRP mapping to improve its competitiveness is Premier Hospital Supply, Inc. (PHS), a medium-sized medical supply company in the United States. Premier's industry is experiencing slowed growth: Sales to hospitals and physicians have decreased as buyers have grown more cautious. Tighter controls imposed by managed care providers have translated into increased pressures for cost containment.[5] In this environment, Premier faced the challenge of reducing costs without reducing customer satisfaction.

Because Premier is a distribution company whose products can be obtained from a number of other distributors, the only way to differentiate itself from its competition is through the services it provides to customers. PHS decided that it needed to focus on those services that provided the most value for its customers. Analysis of its Customer Relationship Process was a promising way to start.

Premier held several two-day meetings with customers to discuss the following:

- The activities of the current Customer Relationship Process
- What the customers perceive as PHS's strengths and weaknesses
- What the customers recommend that PHS do differently

The outcome of the meetings was a preliminary map of the Customer Relationship Process. The map showed six phases, each of which was broken down into distinct activities.

The PHS project team and each sales branch office reviewed the CRP map and suggested improvements. In addition, each region held focus groups with customers to obtain their feedback on the CRP. Said the leader of the CRP team, "We wanted to know what customers expected from a sales rep, from start to finish. Our map is the result of the best ideas from all those who participated."

Among the benefits PHS has seen from the CRP map are improved ability to service its customers, clearer organizational direction, more frequent and open communication with new and existing customers, and a precise focus for sales training.

---

[5]Standard & Poor's Industry Surveys, *Health Care Products and Services* (September 9, 1993), p. 39.

In addition, the work on the CRP led to a change in the company's competitive strategy. The company believed that its needs analysis service, which it offers to customers as a way to define their priorities, was of significant value to customers and was a competitively distinct service. In reviewing the Customer Relationship Process, PHS customers said that the needs analysis step *does*, in fact, provide value. But the customers told PHS that it does not differentiate the company because many of the company's competitors also conduct needs analyses.

Involving customers enabled PHS to gain detailed, current information about what its customers value—and about how its competition was changing to meet those expectations. The company used this information to reevaluate its competitive strategies and identify new ways to differentiate itself.

"We intend to continually update our Customer Relationship Process map to reflect the changing needs of our market," said the executive vice president.

STEWARDSHIP OF THE CUSTOMER RELATIONSHIP PROCESS

"In the future, the best sales managers will be sales process managers."

—Sales manager, Hewlett-Packard Company
(United States)

The many sales organizations that have endorsed the CRP as a core business principle believe that salespeople must be the *stewards of the Customer Relationship Process.* The process may include people from many different functional areas within the organization, but the salesperson remains the customer's primary contact for as long as the relationship lasts.

In fact, AchieveGlobal's research on customer loyalty (discussed in Chapter One) shows that five of the six elements that determine a customer's decision to continue to do business with a supplier organization depend *either directly or indirectly on the salesperson's actions or the expectations he or she creates about the organization.* In North America, the research showed that the salesperson's ability to influence customer loyalty is so strong that "even if customers were unhappy with some aspect of the product performance or service follow-up, the salesperson could keep the relationship intact. This was true *if* the customer felt reassured that the sales organization was ready and able to go the extra mile to restore the relationship."[6]

As the strategic orchestrator of the process, the salesperson needs to know how the CRP will unfold—not just at the sales presentation in the client's office, but also when the customer service rep answers the service call, when the billing clerk generates the invoice, and when the technical expert comes to the client's factory. Whether these people are organized as an account team or working in their own departments, the salesperson can take the initiative to coordinate their efforts.

As a vice president from Océ (The Netherlands) put it, "in the future, everything we sell will be products that are part of a system. Everything will be integrated. This implies that the salesperson has to oversee the total concept instead of just his or her part." Understanding the Customer Relationship Process helps an entire organization focus on the customers' needs; but the sales organization— and specifically, the salesperson—should be the steward of the process on behalf of the organization and its customers.

A PRACTICAL METHOD FOR CRP MAPPING

"From the beginning, we try to help a new representative to create good habits by using the well-established selling process."

—Sales manager, Northwestern Mutual Life Insurance Company
(United States)

Whether an operation defines the entire CRP or merely the subset of activities that directly involve the sales force (SPPM), mapping may not be an easy task. It requires tremendous organizational commitment and discipline. Getting an organization to change on the basis of what the CRP map reveals is even more challenging—especially if the organization already believes itself to be highly successful.

As a vice president from Hewlett-Packard Company (United States) commented, "The biggest challenge is answering the question, 'We are already successful. Why should we change now?' "

Organizations that have documented their CRPs, including AchieveGlobal (see Figure 4-3), offer the following basic guidelines:

---

[6]AchieveGlobal, *Profiles in Customer Loyalty* (1989), p. 9.

FIGURE 4-3
The Customer Relationship Process

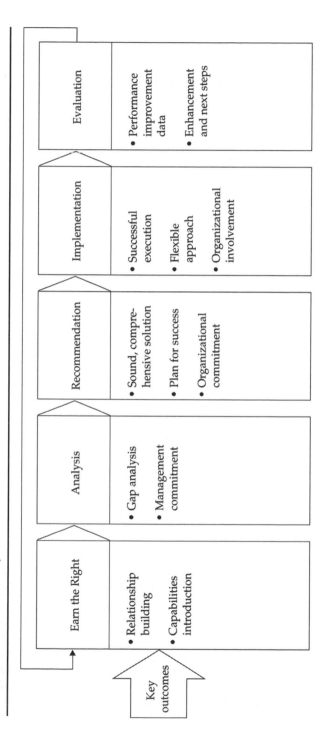

Copyright © 1999, AchieveGlobal

1. *Start with a commitment to better understand and improve how the organization relates to its customers.* The initiative must have a high-level champion, someone who believes in and understands the value of applying quality and business process-management principles to the task of building customer relationships—and who has the authority to make it happen.

2. *Define the phases of the Customer Relationship Process simply and concisely.* An overly complex CRP document will be too cumbersome to use and is more likely to produce confusion than offer guidance.

3. *Anticipate the customer's expectations for each phase.* For example, the customer may expect a salesperson to have in-depth knowledge of the customer's industry.

4. *Define the activities, tools, and resources needed to cost-effectively meet customers' expectations for each phase.* Identify the amount of time and resources that can be devoted to each phase.

5. *Define the performance standards that you will use to assess how well your front-line sales and service professionals meet your customers' expectations.* Most organizations are experimenting with ways to measure sales success over the long *and* short term. A new focus is on measuring sales success with respect to profitability and customer satisfaction, as well as revenue. A salesperson at Scott Paper Company notes that Scott not only measures customers' satisfaction with its products and salespeople but also "their satisfaction with our competitors."

6. *Validate the Customer Relationship Process map with customers.* Solicit customers' input to ensure the usefulness of the activities in the process and the quality of their experiences in each. This will also help ensure buy-in from the front-line sales and service people, who are far more likely to respect a process they know their customers have reviewed and approved. Some companies choose to include customers in the actual creation of the map. This partnership approach involves customers to the fullest and ensures that the process truly meets customer needs.

7. *Gather information from customers about their current and future needs, and examine the competition's strengths and weaknesses with respect to the CRP.* The people who are face to face with customers every day, particularly sales and customer service people, should be involved in analyzing this information to select improvement priorities that take into account the competition's current strengths and weaknesses.

8. *Improve selected activities.* Once the activities of the process are clearly defined, it will be far easier to set priorities for improvement, develop standards, measure and benchmark against those standards, add value, and reduce cost for the selected activities.

9. *Define best practices.* Seek out appropriate models against which to benchmark, whether from within the organization or outside of it. "We are trying to measure what the good salespeople do that the others don't," said a salesperson with 3M (United Kingdom), "to learn lessons from them and teach others."

10. *Use feedback from customers to track progress and identify additional activities to improve.* Once the organization has accepted discussion of the CRP as part of its culture, the likelihood of continuous improvement of standard operating practices increases because of the ability to focus on specific activities and specific feedback. This is critical because of customers' continually escalating demands and today's volatile marketplace conditions.

CONCLUSION

"We now have a focus on customer satisfaction, whereas in the past, it was totally on revenue, profit, or the number of 'net adds.' " [7]

—Vice president, Xerox Corporation
(United States)

The migration of the concepts and techniques of the quality movement into sales organizations has helped many operations to define their goals so that they are consistent with their customers' expectations. It has also helped bring into focus the importance of using customer satisfaction to measure the sales organization's success.

The Customer Relationship Process is another example of a core quality concept that has profound implications for sales organizations. It enables an organization to bring logic, order, and consistency to the everyday actions and behaviors of everyone who interacts with customers. It is an indispensable tool for reengineering all the processes that touch the customer. By identifying the activities that its customers

---

[7]"Net adds" are the number of new units sold minus the number of units replaced. Net adds represent growth over the number of units previously in use.

value most, a sales organization can make decisions based on the *customer's* priorities, not the organization's. When developed properly, the Customer Relationship Process helps organizations identify the activities that, when performed flawlessly, significantly improve their long-term relationships with their most important customers.

BEST PRACTICES AND GUIDING PRINCIPLES

Map your Customer Relationship Process.

- Conduct internal interviews as well as customer interviews, to get a broad description of:
  - The steps in the process
  - The relative value of each to the customer
  - The customer's definition of quality for each step
  - Activities that comprise each step
  - Objective evidence that the step has been completed
- Ensure that the map outlines phases, or stages, as well as activities associated with each phase.
- After mapping the Customer Relationship Process, invite customers to comment on it to verify that it represents the way they want to buy from your organization.

Use your Customer Relationship Process.

- Identify the needs of different markets, and different market segments, as well as how your organization will meet those needs.
- Focus on the CRP in conversations with customers. Ensure that customers understand and provide input on how you will work with them, what they can expect to receive from your organization, and what expectations you can satisfy.
- Identify important competencies, as well as coaching and training needs. Coaching and training decisions should specifically address gaps between "expected" and "actual" performance, as identified in the CRP.
- Develop and enhance your competitive strategy and competitive opportunities. For instance, identify steps in the process that you perform better than your competitors, where you add value and they do not, and vice versa.
- Use customer satisfaction data to evaluate the performance of people in your sales organization.

Chapter Five

Consultative Selling

"In the future, selling will be a balance of customization and standardization. We'll have a portfolio of standard offerings and we'll be able to customize a unique solution to meet each customer's needs. This is the essence of consultative selling."

—Vice president, Scott Paper Company
(United States)

- What is consultative selling?
- How does traditional selling compare with consultative selling?
- What are the elements of strategic problem solving?
- What roles does the consultative salesperson fulfill?
- Is consultative selling a worldwide trend?

The Customer Relationship Process described in Chapter Four is a powerful tool for identifying and improving the activities that establish and strengthen profitable, long-term relationships between your organization and your customers. The knowledge, skills, and attitudes your salespeople use will determine the strength of the relationship between your two organizations.

Sales executives in the leading sales organizations say that the critical skill salespeople need to develop loyal customer partnerships is consultative selling.

The process of consultative selling enables a salesperson and a customer to gain a mutual understanding of the customer's strategic goals and to achieve them by working collaboratively.

Consultative Selling

The process of helping the customer achieve strategic goals through
the use of your product or service.

The key word is *strategic*. With these goals as the basis for the sales conversations, the salesperson and customer can create a highly focused
and targeted solution together. Information flows both ways. Recommendations are based on mutual understanding and agreement.

The customer comes to view the salesperson as an ally—a trusted
advisor and resource—as they work together toward the customer's strategic goal.

Today, more and more customers are eager to participate in this
kind of sales process. "Customers are now disclosing much more
information: They believe that it is in their best interest to be open
and exchange information with our salespeople," reported a vice
president at Xerox Corporation (United States). "They will tell you
what the requirements are and the names of the other suppliers they
are working with. Today's customer/supplier relationships are
built on openness, candor, and trust on both sides."

STRATEGIC PROBLEM SOLVING

"The sales people I value most are problem solvers, not proposal writers."

—Customer, Océ (The Netherlands)

Customers place a high value on salespeople who are able to help
them with strategic problem solving. What a customer describes as
strategic problem solving is what a sales organization thinks of as
consultative selling (see Figure 5–1).

The salesperson who wants to be an effective strategic problem
solver will need the skills and knowledge to be able to:

- Uncover and understand the customer's *strategic needs* by gaining an in-depth knowledge of the customer's organization.
- Develop solutions that demonstrate a *creative* approach to
  addressing the customer's strategic needs in the most efficient
  and effective manner possible.
- Arrive at a *mutually beneficial agreement*.

FIGURE 5-1
Building Customer Relationships

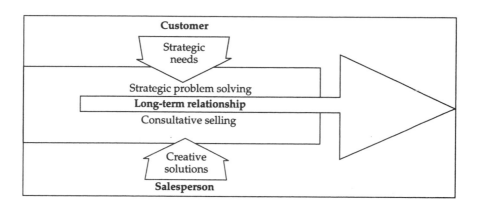

Three key terms in the preceding list—strategic needs, creative solutions, and mutually beneficial agreements—are critical to strategic problem solving.

Strategic Needs

Every customer need has a reason behind it. Usually that reason is another need, or a need behind the need, that represents a strategic goal the customer wants to accomplish.

It might help to think of the customer's range of needs as an onion. The first layer represents the need initially described by the customer. The next layer represents the reason for that initial need—the need behind the need. By peeling away the layers of each need, the salesperson eventually uncovers the core, or strategic, need. The consultative salesperson who understands the full range of the customer's needs is in a much better position to provide a product or service solution that helps the customer progress more efficiently and effectively toward achieving his or her organization's strategic goal.

For example, suppose you're a computer salesperson and one of your prospective customers expresses a need to equip her sales force with laptop computers. The traditional sales approach would be to immediately describe the features and benefits of your line of laptop computers. Using a consultative selling approach, however, you would first explore the reasons the customer wants the computers.

FIGURE 5-2
Need behind the Need

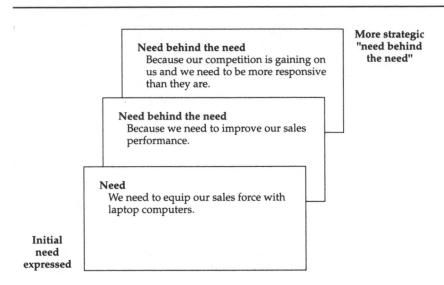

You may find, for instance, that there's a competitive issue: The customer's competition is perceived by the marketplace as more responsive. Therefore, the customer's strategic need is to be more responsive (see Figure 5–2).

Having this information can help you describe the specific aspects of your product line that address the customer's need (to be more responsive) and identify other ways your company might be able to help the customer meet that need. For example, you might offer the services of your company's 24-hour help line or offer to work in partnership with another supplier to develop a customized software program for the new laptops the customer is purchasing from you.

Usually, a need behind the need falls into one of three categories:

- Financial—improving monetary results or controlling costs.
- Image—maintaining or improving prestige.
- Performance—maintaining or improving productivity.

Needs in these strategic areas do not exist in a vacuum; they interrelate and influence each other. That's why top-performing salespeople make sure their probing strategy covers all three areas. As noted earlier, only by understanding and addressing the full scope of the customer's needs can the salesperson recommend a more compre-hensive, long-term solution. When this happens, the salesperson gains not only the customer's increased level of trust and respect, but also an edge—sharpened by his or her knowledge of the cus-tomer's long-term goals—in uncovering new selling opportunities.

"The top salespeople have a breadth of vision," said one vice president at Xerox Corporation (United States). "They can figure out the customer's requirements and come up with a set of specifi-cations that the company can deliver on to meet the requirements. And they can work through complex situations."

Creative Solutions

Each customer is faced with a specific, unique combination of strategic needs and business issues.

As a result, each customer requires a specific solution from the sales organization. The ability of a salesperson to tailor a "custom" solution for each customer is critical today. The salesperson needs to use *creative problem solving* to identify the specific solution that meets each customer's needs.

For most companies in most industries, the competitive necessity to understand and respond to the customer's more complex and strategic needs spells the end of the one-size-fits-all solution. In the past, the *product* was the solution; now, more often than not, the salesperson must create the solution from a mix of products and services. Usually, the solution represents either one of two options:

1. A *customized version or application* of a product and/or service that efficiently addresses the customer's specific strategic needs

2. A *mix of products and services* (including, if appropriate, com-petitors' products and services) that offers the best possible solution in light of the customer's strategic needs

The better a salesperson is at creatively marshaling all available resources to address a customer's strategic need, the stronger the customer relationship becomes. This ability to solve problems cre-atively is one of the characteristics of top salespeople at the leading sales organizations we studied. As a vice president at Scott Paper (United States) described them: "There's a creative energy around getting the answer."

> **Creative Problem Solving**
>
> The ability to develop and combine nontraditional alternatives to meet the specific needs of the customer.

Mutually Beneficial Agreements

Salespeople and customers say that a significant shift has occurred in their expectations of the outcome of sales agreements—from the adversarial "win-lose" to the more collaborative "win-win" arrangement. To achieve a mutually beneficial agreement, salespeople and customers must work together to develop a common understanding of the issues and challenges at hand. Then, together, they can reach a solution that makes sense for both organizations.

To ensure mutual benefit, both parties may agree that, for the time being, the best arrangement is *no* arrangement. This (hopefully) rare circumstance may arise when the salesperson's organization is unable to offer a tenable solution, or the customer's expectations are so high that the sales organization cannot respond to them profitably.

The salesperson's focus on mutually beneficial solutions creates mutual *commitment* to those solutions. This commitment, in turn, enhances the prospects of successfully implementing the solution, thereby strengthening the relationship—and the prospects of doing business together in the future.

Information about an organization's business strategies is often highly confidential. But more and more customers, in the interests of developing solutions that will help achieve their strategic goals, are willing to let salespeople cross the threshold of confidentiality. A customer's willingness or reluctance to share confidential information depends on cultural norms and on the salesperson's ability to develop trust, meet the customer's expectations, and fulfill all the roles of a consultative salesperson.

AN EVOLUTION IN SELLING

"Clients have dramatically changed the way they buy. Salespeople have to adapt to this new situation; they must be advisors to clients."

—Salesperson, Biscuiterie Nantaise (France)

What Do Customers Want?

According to customers, the best salespeople:

- *Are committed to helping their customers succeed.* They know that, to ensure the success of a long-term relationship, they must help their customers achieve long-term objectives.
- *Stay involved with their customers,* even if there is not an immediate sales opportunity.
- *Always focus on the customer's strategic needs* when developing solutions.

Recent decades have brought important changes in selling. Once, the typical sales call was a "pitch"—a presentation focused on a specific product and tightly controlled by the salesperson. Today, the best sales calls are highly interactive dialogues between a salesperson and a customer working toward a common goal.

Sales executives who are thought of as leaders envision the sales call of the future as a balanced exchange of information, based on trust and focused on achieving a mutually beneficial agreement. Their assumption is that the more information—and control—that's shared, the better the solution will be.

Two related developments have paralleled this one. An evolution from selling products, to selling products and services, to selling solutions, has taken place as competitors have caused companies to look for new ways to differentiate. In addition, customer needs have become more complex and more strategic, which makes customers want to do business with sales organizations that can help them meet those needs.

Taken together, these trends represent an evolution from traditional selling to consultative selling, as described in Table 5–1.

THREE ROLES OF CONSULTATIVE SELLING

"We must take the business and sales status of each retailer into account, and guide and instruct each one concerning the additional value of each product."

—Salesperson, Shiseido Company (Japan)

TABLE 5-1
Comparison of Traditional and Consultative Selling

	Traditional Selling	*Consultative Selling*
Role of salesperson	"Lone ranger"	Strategic orchestrator Business consultant Long-term ally Key player in the customer's business
Involvement of customer and salesperson	Minimum customer involvement; maximum salesperson involvement	Heavy involvement of both customer and salesperson
Information flow	One-way: salesperson to customer	Two-way
Focus of interaction	Product/service features and applications	Ability of the solution to address the need behind the need— such as the customer's improved financial performance

Knowledge required	Own company's
	    Products and services
	
	    Competitors
	    Applications
	
	    Account strategy
	    Costs
	    Opportunities
		General business and industry trends
		
		Own company's
		    Products and services
		    Competitors
		    Applications
		    Account strategy
		    Costs
		    Opportunities
		
		Customer's
		    Products and services
		    Competitors
		    Customers

Skills required	Face-to-face selling skills	Face-to-face selling skills, including in-depth probing Strategic problem-solving

TABLE 5-1
Comparison of Traditional and Consultative Selling (Continued)

		Demonstrating how solutions meet strategic objectives
		Team-building and teamwork
Salesperson's involvement in customer's decision-making process	Uninvolved Isolated from decision-making process	Involved
Salesperson's involvement after purchase and installation	Very little: "hit and run"; move on to the next customer	Salesperson continues to call on customer organization to ensure successful long-term performance
		Salesperson directs the activities of the Customer Relationship Process throughout sales and service cycles

The evolution from traditional selling to consultative selling requires salespeople to be more versatile, creative, and visionary than ever before.

To help sales organizations understand—and become proficient at—selling consultatively, AchieveGlobal conducted a two-phase research study designed to determine what effective and less-effective salespeople do differently. [1] The research results helped define consultative selling on a more practical level.

---

[1]For an explanation of this study, see "Roles of the Salesperson" research in Appendix B.

FIGURE 5-3
Three Roles of the Consultative Salesperson

The first phase of the study investigated the types of behaviors that characterize the most successful salespeople. Results of this phase revealed several major findings, which were consistent across industries:

These findings suggest that salespeople need to fulfill all three roles to be effective at consultative selling. (See Figure 5-3.)

The second phase of research identified specific practices associated with each of the three roles. These practices are included in the "Best Practices and Guiding Principles" sections at the end of Chapters 6, 7, and 8.

We'll examine each of these roles in detail in the following three chapters. In the meantime, the following paragraphs offer a quick overview.

In the role of strategic orchestrator, survey respondents said the salesperson works to harness all of his or her company's resources for the customer, seeking assistance from others and building cooperation.

The salesperson involves colleagues at all levels of the organization and adopts a problem-solving approach to production, delivery implementation, and service concerns. The salesperson is also able to weigh the costs and benefits of various value-adding activities and make the customer aware of them in a way that builds the business relationship.

As an effective business consultant, the salesperson uses internal and external resources to gain an understanding of the customer's business and marketplace. The salesperson thoroughly educates the customer about the products he or she offers, as well as how they compare with competitors' offerings. The salesperson has well-thought-out plans for his or her territory and for each account. He or she approaches problem solving and decision making with creativity and an understanding of the "big picture."

In the role of long-term ally, the salesperson acts as a business partner, working to support the customer even when there is no immediate prospect for a sale. He or she positions products and services honestly and turns down business that isn't in the customer's long-term interest. The salesperson "goes to bat" for customers whenever necessary and helps customers carry out fact-finding missions within their own companies. In addition, the salesperson shows pride in his or her company, products, and services.

Many organizations have found they need to train their salespeople to recognize the value of the individual roles and the way the three roles interact to create a long-term bond with customers.

The findings of this study make a connection between the three roles and today's business realities, including the increased emphasis on service and escalating customer expectations. The research demystifies the often nebulous notion of consultative selling and creates an observable link between the three roles and quota performance. It also suggests that top sales professionals have evolved far beyond supplier status in the eyes of their customers.

CONCLUSION

Sales executives from all industries and all countries say that the ability to develop long-term relationships with their customers will be critical to the success of their business in the future—and that the ability of their salespeople to be consultative will be an essential factor in achieving this goal.

As a sales manager at Siemens (Germany) said, "Each salesperson must have an understanding of how the market has changed, so he or she can invest the appropriate activity and energy in the right place."

Consultatively Speaking

The following are selected quotes from our sales leadership research on the subject of consultative selling.

- "Successful people will be the ones who understand their company's strategy. This will be true for salespeople and for customers."
- "Needs-based selling will continue to evolve so that we are truly focused on the customer's business goals and total system needs."
- We used to sell products; now we sell solutions."
- "We are pushing our salespeople to see themselves as consultants and sales professionals."
- "Our vision is for our salespeople to understand the business problems of the account, to know how to get to high levels, and to develop relationships."
- "We can help our customers look at the business in a different way. We can help them get a product to market faster by examining the steps in the process and telling them how to reduce the steps. It's a question of document flow—it's not a question of selling a copier."
- "Salespeople can help customers find new ways to solve business problems, to look further than price and features. We want the account to look at us as more than the seller of the box; we want to help them look at utilization and the bigger issues."

The term *consultative selling* is not a new one, but these sales executives are redefining it to reflect the values of today's more sophisticated customers and the abilities of today's more sophisticated sales forces.

The next three chapters describe the three roles of consultative selling. A complete understanding of each of these roles—strategic orchestrator, business consultant, and long-term ally—is critical to fulfilling this vision.

BEST PRACTICES AND GUIDING PRINCIPLES

- When gathering information, analyzing data, and recommending solutions, the focus should be on the customer's *strategic* needs— the needs behind the needs that may have been initially expressed. Key to this is a probing strategy that uncovers issues related to financial, image, or performance needs.

- Salespeople have to earn the right to be seen as consultative salespeople. Their first challenge is to build credibility. They achieve this by demonstrating integrity, reliability, and expertise.

- Customers say that sales organizations should give salespeople the authority to make important decisions independently. This allows them to meet customer needs promptly, and gain customers' trust and respect.

- Salespeople should be able to provide creative solutions to strategic problems in an efficient and effective manner. To do this, sales organizations should be set up to provide customized, nontraditional applications of products or services. Combinations of products or services, even including those of competitors, may be needed.

Chapter Six

Salesperson as Strategic Orchestrator

"In the future, salespeople will work on multifunctional teams. There won't be any more 'Lone Rangers.'"

—Vice president, Scott Paper Company
(United States)

- What is a "strategic orchestrator"?
- What does the strategic orchestrator do for the customer?
- What practices and competencies are associated with the strategic orchestrator role?
- What is team selling? Why is it an example of the strategic orchestrator role?
- What leads to successful team selling?

In response to customers' escalating expectations and increasingly complex problems, successful salespeople have learned to draw on the full range of resources of their organizations. Figure 6-1 shows the three roles of the consultative salesperson. Fulfilling all three consultative roles enables salespeople to manage the information explosion that confronts them, while developing partnerships that benefit their own organizations as well as their customers.

This chapter discusses the role of strategic orchestrator and its relationship to effective team selling. Chapters 7 and 8 will examine the other two roles of the consultative salesperson: business consultant and long-term ally.

FIGURE 6–1
Three Roles of the Consultative Salesperson

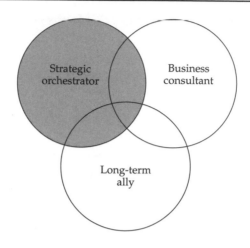

REVOLUTION IN BUSINESS RELATIONSHIPS: FROM ONE-ON-ONE TO ORGANIZATION-TO-ORGANIZATION

As customers' needs become more and more complex, many customer organizations have set up *buying teams* to ensure that their organizations accurately convey their complex needs and thoroughly assess the accuracy of suppliers' recommendations. In addition, they demand more information, ideas, and resources from sales organizations so they can address these needs and achieve their goals.

There was a time when customers were content to work with a single contact from a supplier organization. Very often, the salesperson was the *only* person from his or her organization whom the customer knew. Today, however, fewer and fewer customers are comfortable with this arrangement. Customers want access to a supplier's full range of resources. Furthermore, if they are going to share strategic information to address the ever-widening scope of their business challenges, customers want the assurance that an *organization,* not a single individual, is committed to the relationship.

Leading sales organizations are *equally* uncomfortable with having a single point of contact between the customer and their organization. Sales organizations realize that they are unable to ade-

---

Strategic Orchestrator

A salesperson who coordinates all of the information, resources, and activities needed to support customers before, during, and after the sale.

---

quately meet the customer's needs and expectations if only one person is working with the account. And if they don't meet those needs, a more responsible competitor will. They recognize that customers expect their supplier relationships to involve more than just contact between one salesperson and one buyer. In addition, there is the danger of losing the business and losing the account information and relationship if the salesperson leaves the assignment.

As business relationships evolve from one-on-one to organization-to-organization, a critical part of the salesperson's new role is to ensure that establishing and sustaining customer relationships is perceived as everyone's responsibility—not just the salesperson's.

STRATEGIC ORCHESTRATORS: STEWARDS OF THE PARTNERSHIP

"Our best salespeople are team captains, not individual stars."

—Sales manager, Hewlett-Packard Company
(United States)

A fundamental change in the role of the salesperson is to serve as the primary contact between the two organizations and to make the customer aware of the network of resources that stands behind the salesperson. The best will assume the role of strategic orchestrator. Strategic orchestrators harness *all* their company's resources for their customers. They know whom to contact, and how to manage their involvement, so that they can put together unique solutions for customers or address their production, delivery, or service concerns. Observed a salesperson for Boehme Chemie (Germany), "I *manage* these accounts; I do not merely sell to them."

In their role as strategic orchestrators, salespeople are stewards of their organization's partnership with the customer. They make sure they are kept informed about—and have the opportunity to influence—every significant customer contact with their organization, whether at the supplier organization's inbound telemarketing center, field office, warehouse, customer service department, or the client's receiving dock and installation site. When appropriate, top salespeople create additional activities—and involve people from different functional areas or with different expertise or authority—to optimize the customer's experience and ensure that the organization delivers what the customer values.

As a vice president from Iron Trades Insurance Group (United Kingdom) remarked, "Linking service and sales is important to build relationships; there is no longer just one person selling the business. We are selling the whole company."

WHAT A STRATEGIC ORCHESTRATOR IS —AND DOES

The salespeople who best fulfill the role of strategic orchestrator, and therefore sell consultatively, will, according to AchieveGlobal's research, be people who have mastered six key competencies. These competencies are:

1. Knowledge of their own company's structure
2. Expertise in building and managing a team
3. Ability to manage priorities and performance
4. Ability to coordinate delivery and service to their customers
5. Efficiency
6. Flexibility

The specific practices associated with each of these competencies are discussed in the following paragraphs.

Knowledge of their own company's structure. Salespeople who fulfill the role of strategic orchestrator have a comprehensive understanding of their company's mission, markets, products, and competitors. They are familiar with their organization's policies and procedures, with how the different departments operate, and with who has the power to make key decisions. They also know who in their company communicates most effectively with clients and who is more effective "behind the scenes." As a sales training supervisor

---

Northwestern Mutual Life: The Hidden Dimension of Service

At Northwestern Mutual Life Insurance Company (United States), agents frequently draw on the resources of a "hidden dimension" of the organization: the attorneys and other specialists who serve the policy owners behind the scenes, although they never meet them. These people provide advice to the selling agent about the solutions and programs the agent has designed, to ensure that they are based on sound legal and financial principles and current laws.

"What do your top agents do that is different from what your average performers do?" we asked. A sales manager responded, "Hard work, smart work, team work."

---

from 3M (United Kingdom) commented when asked about what it will take to succeed in selling in the future, "It's not just selling skills or relationship building that will be important. Salespeople will have to be able to manage the resources available to them." Said a customer of Tokio Marine and Fire Insurance (Japan), "The truly excellent salesperson sells by effectively utilizing internal resources."

Expertise in building and managing a team. Strategic orchestrators realize that to meet the expectations of today's customers, they need the cooperation of others within their own organization. For that reason, they develop knowledge of the organization's "political structure" and maintain good working relationships with superiors, colleagues, and support staff. They use excellent communications skills to build a team that is willing and able to meet customer needs. Their ability to manage this team throughout the selling process and beyond quite simply makes salespeople more productive. "Top salespeople know how to delegate," observed a sales manager from Northwestern Mutual Life Insurance Company (United States).

Ability to manage priorities and performance. Along with their ability to manage a team, strategic orchestrators are able to manage their own priorities to achieve continuous performance improvement. They assign a priority to every task and invest their time appropriately. They know how to establish realistic, but challenging, personal performance goals and achieve them by setting specific, short-term objectives. "Top salespeople achieve goals that are based on their own clear vision," noted an area sales manager for Sony Corporation (Japan). Because they monitor their progress, they know when there's a problem, and they can develop a specific action plan to remedy the situation. They constantly seek feedback from others on ways to improve their personal performance.

Ability to coordinate delivery and service to their customers. Strategic orchestrators are committed to their customers' satisfaction, even after a sale has been made. As a vice president from Xerox Corporation (United States) observed, "Top salespeople are concerned about total customer satisfaction and have the desire to make sure that everything is going right with the customer." To ensure customer satisfaction, strategic orchestrators coordinate all aspects of product and service delivery, making sure that the customer understands what is happening at every step. They do not limit their interactions with customers to sales calls; they maintain high visibility even when others within their company are working directly with the customer. They also determine if any additional resources are needed to serve the customer—and when, where, and how to obtain them.

Efficiency. "Strategic orchestrators spend a lot of time planning what they need to do to achieve goals so they don't waste time," said a sales manager from Iron Trades Insurance Group (United Kingdom). They maintain an efficient sales record-keeping system, complete routine paperwork on time, and make sure their administrative activities do not interfere with customer-related tasks.

Flexibility. Effective strategic orchestrators are able to adapt well to a wide variety of situations. They are comfortable juggling priorities and responsibilities, selling a variety of products and services, and working under deadline pressures to meet requests and expectations of multiple customers. As a vice president from Xerox Corporation (United States) commented candidly, "Top salespeople are mature enough to work through the problems and always focus on the customer's requirements."

Team Selling

When a team from the supplier organization meets with a potential or existing customer with the intention of advancing a sales cycle and building a business relationship.

Customers of strategic orchestrators have a high level of confidence in the salesperson and in the salesperson's organization. As a customer of Océ (The Netherlands) put it, "The way the salesperson mobilized his sales organization and eventually solved the problem left me feeling, 'With this guy, I can do business.' " This increased confidence can lead to faster purchase decisions, increased repeat business, and strengthened bonds between customer and supplier organizations.

Top-performing organizations recognize that the salesperson, in the role of strategic orchestrator, can make invaluable contributions to team-based initiatives. For example, at Union Pacific Railroad (United States) the national account managers are the customers' primary contacts. They coordinate the efforts of others and lead teams from a wide range of departments to solve problems, identify quality- and satisfaction-improvement opportunities, and strengthen the relationship between customers and Union Pacific.

Strategic orchestrators put these practices to good use in organizations both large and small—whether they orchestrate the aspects of the partnership across time zones or simply across town. Sometimes, it may be appropriate for the customer to remain unaware of the salesperson's role in coordinating people, products, and information. At other times, the salesperson's demonstrated ability to put an array of resources at the customer's disposal is what cements the business relationship. One of the ways that salespeople use their abilities as strategic orchestrators most visibly is through team selling.

AN EXAMPLE OF STRATEGIC ORCHESTRATION: TEAM SELLING

As discussed earlier, customers today look for salespeople and their organizations to demonstrate greater depth and breadth of knowledge about the customers' businesses. Team selling is one way to achieve this expectation by bringing resources and information—in the form of the people who are best prepared to answer the customer's questions or concerns—into an actual sales call.

It may take place over the phone, in person, or even by video teleconference. Regardless of venue, the purpose of team selling is to advance the sales cycle by bringing appropriate players from the supplier organization into a sales discussion with a potential or existing customer.

Team selling can differentiate the sales organization by quickly providing customers with a wide range of information, advice, ideas, and even decisions. No more "Let me get back to you on that," or "Why don't I have one of our engineers give you a call?" The supplier organization can use team selling as a mechanism for providing customers with answers quickly and efficiently.

Fuji Xerox (Japan) has used team selling for many years as a key element of its strategy to build long-term relationships with customers. The salesperson coordinates the involvement of members of the technical staff, marketing staff, and others to ensure that customers are fully informed about the capabilities and applications of the most up-to-date equipment.

Involving people with different personalities and communication styles in a sales call is particularly advantageous for addressing a wide range of issues or for reinforcing key points. As a salesperson at Allen & Hanbury's (United Kingdom) said, "One person might be able to deal more effectively with certain aspects of the call, or certain customer attitudes, and another person can deal more effectively with others. Also, it adds credibility when you are backing up each other's statements."

From the point of view of the supplier organization, the presence of several people on a sales call provides the opportunity to view the sales interaction from a variety of perspectives. The participants in a team sales call can obtain more relevant and accurate information than a lone salesperson ever could. The salesperson—or team—can then use that information to plan more efficiently and develop better strategies. The bottom-line impact is improved sales productivity.

What do customers think about team selling? They say that team selling has many advantages. It helps them:

- Ensure that their concerns are heard and their needs are met
- Obtain a bigger picture of the products, services, and solutions that the supplier organization has to offer
- Determine whether (or how well) the different departments of the supplier organization work together
- Obtain customized recommendations that mesh with strategic business goals
- Reach better and faster agreements on price, deliverables, and terms and conditions

- Exchange vital technical and business information with their counterparts in other companies

As a customer of Océ (The Netherlands) summed it up, "Team selling gives me the opportunity to get commitments from the people who are responsible for different activities."

Although large corporations have set many of the precedents for team selling, authors Cespedes, Doyle, and Freedman point out that it can be as useful to the three-person consulting firm as it is to the multinational conglomerate.[1] In fact, the relevance of team selling for a particular situation often has far more to do with the *customer's* needs than with the size or structure of the supplier organization. Consider three of the applications in which team selling is most effective: high-technology solutions, warehouse/superstore sales, and global solutions.

Team selling is a critical tool for organizations that market high-technology products. Constant advancements in high technology make it difficult for a single salesperson to remain up to date on new developments. Leading sales organizations find that teams of people can more easily satisfy customers who have complex challenges, needs, and expectations. "As you move from single products into more sophisticated systems, team selling is the only way to go: Technical support people, administrative support people, and installation people all have to work together to meet the customer's requirements," said a sales manager from Xerox Corporation (United States).

Team selling is essential to developing appropriate broad-based solutions. As a vice president from Hewlett-Packard Company (United States) observed, "The resource-intensive sale demands leaders who manage all the team members." Another reason these companies turn to team selling is because installation, service, and support have become so critical; the customer demands evidence of how both the salesperson *and* the behind-the-scenes team will service the account after the sale. Customers say that team selling is a service-oriented activity that sets a company apart from its competition.

---

[1]Frank V. Cespedes, Stephen X. Doyle, and Robert J. Freedman, "Teamwork for Today's Selling," *Harvard Business Review* (March–April 1989).

Another type of organization that often profits from team selling is warehouse stores—operations that sell items in bulk quantities from groceries to housewares in bulk to consumers. The success of these superstores depends on their buying power, which is backed by sophisticated inventory, availability, and delivery tracking systems. Teams from the retailers expect to work with teams from supplier organizations to get better service and lower prices. The coordinated, team-sell approach is crucial, particularly in cases where suppliers sell multiple products through different sales forces.

Team selling is also important among organizations that have a growing number of multinational customers. The complex problems associated with crossing geographical and organizational boundaries, managing different currencies, and achieving multiple objectives require both savvy team leadership and intense team participation.

MAKING TEAM SELLING WORK

For all its benefits, team selling does present some formidable challenges. First among these is the issue of compensation. Unless they are compensated for their contributions, many potential members of a sales team may be unwilling to devote time and effort to helping salespeople sell.

As one district sales manager put it bluntly, "I've got monthly numbers to meet with limited time and resources. I don't get paid or recognized for helping someone else sell. So I don't do it."[2]

Salespeople may also be unwilling to share the rewards of making the sale. In other instances, the costs of drawing several people together to meet with the client can provoke skepticism about the impact of team selling on overall profitability.

Organizations that use team selling successfully have suggested these guidelines:

1. *Drive it from the top.* Communication of the organization's strategic goals and the salespeople's role in achieving them is critical. When team selling is one of the organization's tactics

---

[2]Cespedes et al., pp. 44–48.

for achieving key goals, it has to be made a priority and endorsed at all levels of the organization—starting with the
chief executive officer.

2. *Set clear criteria and goals.* Team selling should be used only
   for those customer situations that warrant it. When it is the
   chosen tactic, it should be guided by specific, measurable
   sales objectives and monitored for its effectiveness.

3. *Select an appropriate team structure.* A team's organizational
   structure influences its level of success. Different structures
   include *creative* teams, set up to optimize autonomy and *tacti-
   cal* teams used to execute a plan.[3] Whatever organizational
   structure is used, everyone on the team must clearly under-

---

Team Selling at Hewlett-Packard Company

Team selling is widely used now at Hewlett-Packard Company (HP)
(United States), but it wasn't always this way. Until the late 1980s,
HP's salespeople marketed primarily to management information
systems (MIS) people, who, at the time, made the purchase decisions
for their companies.

However, as their knowledge and expectations expanded, HP's
clients began making buying decisions at higher levels in the organization. HP salespeople found that, although they still held the custom-
ary technical conversations with their MIS contacts, they now had to
justify purchases with the client's financial representatives and explain
to its executives what the technology would do for their company.

It became clear that a lone Hewlett-Packard representative could
not expect to attend a sales meeting and have at his or her fingertips
all the data the customer needed. To address the knowledge deficit,
HP salespeople began to bring experts with them to talk about the
technical details while they discussed how the proposed product applications would address the customer's specific business issues.

Over time, team selling took on form and substance. The company
began to map the sales process so they could replicate it and expand
upon the team selling experience. Building on the lessons they
learned from their manufacturing quality initiative, HP management established customer feedback systems and developed the
team selling procedures the organization uses today.

---

[3]Cespedes et al., pp. 44–48.

stand his or her role on the team— and should be held accountable for fulfilling that role.

4. *Compensate team members appropriately.* All the other measures to promote team selling will be in vain without an equitable compensation system. Common compensation solutions include establishing a bonus pool and sharing sales credit.

5. *Train team members for continuing success.* To ensure the success of team selling, top-performing organizations train team members in selling skills, interpersonal communication skills, and teamwork.

Xerox Corporation (United States), for example, considers training in interpersonal communication skills to be critical to the success of its team selling efforts. "We know that we have to work together effectively as teams," says a manager in the U.S. marketing group.

A Salesperson's Checklist for Successful Team Selling

Before you meet with a customer,
- Decide on an objective for the sales call that describes the internal resources required. Include funding needed, computer time, type of personnel, etc.
- Describe the team selling process to the customer so he or she understands the value the team will add.
- Designate a team leader to manage the team. This doesn't have to be the salesperson. The individual with the most knowledge in the area of focus (based on the objective) could manage the work of the team.
- Identify each team member's role. Be sure to include individuals in the customer organization as well as your own.
- Define, specifically, how each individual's role will help the customer.
- Determine a process for sales calls.
- Practice (and practice again) the process for the sales call.

After the sales call,
- Conduct a debriefing session among the team members to share observations and ideas.
- Review commitments.
- Determine an action plan.
- Monitor the implementation and success of the action plan.

"From sales, administration, and service—all of us are taught inter-personal communication skills so we can work together more effec-tively to meet the customer's needs."

Salespeople may initially be uncomfortable with team selling. However, they grow to accept and appreciate the change for one very simple reason: Team selling helps them sell better. "I was un-comfortable when I was introduced to team selling," said one sales-person. "But when I realized I just couldn't sell the product on my own, I learned to like it."

CONCLUSION

Customers today look for suppliers that can demonstrate much greater depth and breadth of knowledge about their businesses and the ability to deliver well-thought-out, customized, comprehensive solutions to their business challenges. Like symphony conductors, salespeople must be able to bring in the proper resources at the right time and coordinate the efforts of a number of people within both the customer and supplier organizations. They must accomplish this while ensuring that the customer's personal and organizational needs are met. Salespeople who excel as strategic orchestrators will create bonds with customers that are not easily broken.

BEST PRACTICES AND GUIDING PRINCIPLES

Encourage your salespeople to take on the role of strategic orches-trator through the following practices:

- Involve your company's decision makers in the customer's business.
- Know the responsibilities of colleagues who are not salespeople.
- Know the strengths and shortcomings of colleagues.
- Coordinate the efforts of colleagues in all functions.
- Maintain rapport with managers.
- Seek assistance or guidance from others in the company.
- Adopt a problem-solving approach to production, delivery, and service problems.
- Anticipate the customer's concerns, and initiate the coordination necessary to satisfy the customer's current and future needs.

- Weigh the costs and benefits associated with various value-adding activities, and assert the value of personal time and effort.
- Initiate the coordination necessary to meet the customer's needs.
- Facilitate communication between customers and the company's own research and development, sales management, or customer support personnel.

Assess whether team selling should be a practice in your organization. Ask yourself the following:

- Is team selling consistent with our organization's culture?
- What do we hope to accomplish through team selling? How will it add value for our customers?
- What has our experience with team selling been? Under what conditions has it been helpful? What are some of the lessons learned?
- Do our competitors use team selling? What do we know about their success with it?

When integrating team selling into your organization,

- Communicate to all employees the reasons behind the shift to team selling, what you hope to accomplish with it, and how it will benefit your organization and customers.
- Identify changes in your operations, processes, and organizational structure that would create an environment more conducive to team selling.
- Identify and address factors that might inhibit the success of team selling. These include attitudes, structural barriers, communication channels, procedures, and policies.
- Find ways to implement team selling systematically. Team selling should be a focus of training and coaching, as well as measurement and reward systems.

Ensure that:

- Top management gives recognizable support to team selling. This includes recognition and rewards for executing it effectively and allocation of funding for training.
- Everyone in the organization sees the value in team selling, is clear about the organization's team selling goal, and is committed to its success.

Chapter Seven

Salesperson as Business Consultant

"The essential role of a salesperson is selling. But salespeople also need to be advisors: They must offer clients a full package of advice and service."

—Sales manager, Matra Communications
(France)

- How do salespeople fulfill the role of business consultant?
- What practices and competencies are associated with this role?
- What information do salespeople need to be effective business consultants?
- How can you ensure that your salespeople have the right information?
- Why are electronic performance support systems important?

As we have seen from AchieveGlobal's research and discussion of the changing marketplace, customers expect more from salespeople than ever before. Beginning with the first interaction between a salesperson and customer, the customer looks for evidence of the salesperson's general business knowledge and ability to ask insightful, "big picture" questions about the customer's business needs and objectives. Figure 7-1 reviews the relationship among the three roles of a salesperson.

"Customers want to work with salespeople who are aware of the fast-moving business environment and are able to offer up-to-date advice," said a customer of BP Oil (The Netherlands). Most salespeople are aware of this customer expectation. Many talk about the

FIGURE 7–1
The Three Roles of the Consultative Salesperson

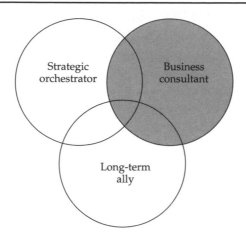

importance of "earning the right" to continue the sales discussions at each meeting. One respondent in the AchieveGlobal study said that his first task as a salesperson was to "get the customer to buy *me.*" In other words, before salespeople can sell a product or service, they must first sell themselves—they must persuade the customers of their integrity, reliability, and ability to understand needs and recommend effective solutions.

Salespeople can demonstrate integrity and reliability by providing solid insights into the customer's business challenges and then offering straightforward guidance about the best way to meet those challenges. In so doing, the salesperson transcends the role of a supplier and becomes a trusted business advisor.

Our research of top sales organizations around the world reveals three factors that have the most influence on a salesperson's ability to fulfill the role of business consultant. Those three factors are:

- Knowledge
- Communication skills
- Attitude

In this chapter, we'll examine these factors and describe how they can help your salespeople step more easily into the role of business consultant. We'll also look at how information management systems can enhance the effectiveness of any business consultant's approach.

Business Consultant

A salesperson who fosters customer confidence and strengthens selling relationships by demonstrating:

- General business knowledge
- A comprehensive understanding of the customer's business challenges
- An ability to develop and help implement effective solutions and recommendations.

KNOWLEDGE: BEYOND PRODUCTS AND SERVICES

"A salesperson must have the capacity and the intellect to absorb a tremendous amount of information and turn it into action that yields results quickly."

—Sales manager, Xerox Corporation
(United States)

Because customers today are under pressure to accomplish more objectives using fewer resources, a growing number rely on salespeople to help them make effective business decisions. But there's a catch: Most customers don't have time to educate salespeople about their organization. Today they expect salespeople to come to the very first meeting prepared to discuss some of the deeper issues surrounding the customer's organization. Because customers have more supplier options available, they are impatient with salespeople who are unable to quickly demonstrate that they are knowledgeable business professionals and not simply persuasive "peddlers."

This is one of the greatest challenges salespeople face today. To add value for their customers, salespeople need to know a significant amount about the customer's business at the start of every sales interaction. In other words, they have to know *more* when they walk in the door.

Top sales professionals become knowledgeable business consultants by:

1. *Demonstrating and refining their understanding of the customer's big-picture challenges and bottom-line realities.* "With both new and existing customers," said a salesperson with Northwestern Mutual Life Insurance Company (United States), "the

---

Information for Competitive Advantage: Hewlett-Packard

Hewlett-Packard Company (United States) is an example of an organization that uses information to add value to its customer relationships. Since its customers deal with high-technology issues, they have extremely high technical literacy and sophistication. To ensure its salespeople can be business consultants to these customers, Hewlett-Packard provides its salespeople with tools to learn as much about their clients as about the technology they sell.

Before they walk into a sales call, salespeople have conducted a thorough analysis of the customer. This analysis also involves becoming intimately familiar with other suppliers' products and how they might be integrated with Hewlett-Packard products. Armed with this knowledge, Hewlett-Packard salespeople are able to build a solution that involves complementary products from its many partners, and, when necessary, technological pieces from competitive companies. This is evidence of HP's commitment to help its customers find the best solutions.

---

salesperson must constantly be in tune with what the customer is thinking about." Effective business consultants at first set aside the question of potential for their own products and services. Instead, they use all resources and contacts available to gain a comprehensive understanding of:

- The issues at all levels of the customer's organization, including strategic, departmental, and individual needs
- The customer's perceptions of market trends, company direction, and potential product and service needs

"Salespeople should have good knowledge of what is happening in the market and how their products can help customers keep up with the changes and evolutions," remarked a customer of BP Oil (The Netherlands). "Customers need up-to-date advice."

2. *Fostering the exchange of information and ideas.* Business consultants facilitate the free flow of information and ideas between their organization and their customers' organizations. As part of this effort, salespeople need to

- Take the time needed to familiarize their customers with their own industry and company.

- Share useful business information with customers, even when the information doesn't directly further their sales effort.
- Demonstrate the cost-cutting or revenue-producing benefits of their products and services.

3. *Continually strengthening their business knowledge.* Business consultants make a point of staying current with the business world at large, not just their own, or even their customers', particular field of specialization. They constantly look for the business trends that influence their customers' organizations, and any new opportunities these trends may offer toward helping their customers become more successful. To keep abreast of these trends, business consultants:

- Read newspapers, magazines, journals, trade publications, annual reports, and other sources of business information
- Maintain memberships in appropriate professional organizations
- Acknowledge gaps in their understanding or knowledge and then take steps to fill these gaps by soliciting information from appropriate sources
- Locate or develop online or offline databases containing information on customers, their industries, and their customers

COMMUNICATION SKILLS: BEYOND PERSUASION

"Communication skills are a must. I can't think of a good salesperson who doesn't know how to talk to people."

—Sales manager, Hewlett-Packard Company
(United States)

In addition to being knowledgeable business professionals, effective business consultants are skilled communicators. No matter how brilliant and knowledgeable a salesperson may be, the information he or she brings to the sales call is useful to the customer only if the salesperson is able to express it clearly and in a way the customer understands and values.

This is not simply the ability to use compelling words when introducing or describing a product or service. Respondents in the sales leadership study said that the communication skills they value most in salespeople are the ability to ask effective questions, listen and demonstrate understanding, and express themselves clearly. Salespeople who fulfill the role of business consultant continually do the following:

1. *Sharpen their approach to identifying customers' needs.* Business consultants develop and continually fine-tune their ability to uncover customer needs. As a result they are able to develop solutions that make sense for their customers' immediate and long-term objectives.

   A critical element in uncovering and analyzing customer needs is asking the right questions. In addition, salespeople need to be able to direct the discussion to focus on the customer's priorities and interests. Salespeople must actively listen to customers' comments to confirm their understanding of customers' needs and to determine customers' level of satisfaction with current products or services. In some cases, the salesperson helps customers identify needs that they may not realize they have. This is often the case when the product or service is complex or intangible. "In retail, people walk into a store and know what they need to buy," explained a sales manager with Northwestern Mutual Life Insurance Company (United States). "In our business, they may not even know that they have a need." Top salespeople never stop asking questions; they never presume that they understand the customer's business so well that they don't need to constantly check their assumptions, especially when developing solutions. Successful business consultants should:

- Confirm their understanding of each customer's mission, goals, strategies, markets, products and services, business functions, and competitors.
- Find out what customers must do to succeed in their jobs.

2. *Refine their communication skills.* Effective business consultants are always looking for ways to enhance communication skills that enable them to develop, explain, and implement solutions. They constantly:

- Speak at listeners' levels of knowledge and sophistication.
- Use stories and analogies effectively.
- Ask for feedback from customers on the clarity of their communication.

3. *Polish their presentation skills.* The ability to effectively present the recommended solution to the customer is critical. "Salespeople have to be good at presenting a package once they understand what the customer requires," said a sales manager at Allen & Hanbury's (United Kingdom). For example, during most presentations, the salesperson must be able to:

- Describe the sales organization's capabilities.
- Introduce new or improved products and services.
- Make a proposal or offer a recommendation.
- Create a common understanding and/or facilitate an agreement among a group of buyers or decision makers.
- Gain the customer's agreement to buy or to take the next step in the sales process.

The clarity of the salesperson's presentation is the proof for the customer of how well the salesperson understands his or her needs. The logic and persuasiveness of the recommendation demonstrate the salesperson's ability to guide customers in achieving their desired objective.

ATTITUDE: BEYOND POSITIVE THINKING

"Skills can be developed over time, but the right attitude has to be there from the beginning."

—Sales manager, Northwestern Mutual Life Insurance Company (United States)

Have you ever met a salesperson whose knowledge and eloquence were dazzling . . . but whose attitude irritated you so much that it sabotaged any chance of a relationship between your two organizations?

The "right" attitude goes beyond the positive thinking that has characterized traditional how-to sales literature and speeches. According to the sales and customer organizations interviewed, the more effective business consultants are characterized in these ways:

- *"They are sensitive and perceptive."*

—Sales manager, Xerox Corporation (United States)

- *"They are more like colleagues to us than salespeople."*

—Customer, Boehme (Germany)

- *"They are motivated more by the intrinsic rewards than the extrinsic ones.*

—Sales manager, Northwestern Mutual Life Insurance Company
(United States)

- *"They are able to give up preconceived attitudes. Flexibility is their way of thinking."*

—Sales manager, Bayerische Vereinsbank (Germany)

- *"They are always enthusiastic. They think around the situation and know how to turn a problem into an opportunity."*

—Sales manager, Allen & Hanbury's
(United Kingdom)

- *"They have high integrity. They are ethical and professional."*

—Sales manager, Scott Paper Company
(United States)

- *"They achieve goals that are based on their own clear vision."*

—Area sales manager, Sony Corporation (Japan)

For all the discussion about business sophistication, the "right" attitude is still a critical element of successful selling.

THE INFORMATION REVOLUTION COMES TO SELLING

"Selling is changing in two ways. First, it's becoming more consultative, which means bringing in a team with the right technical expertise, identifying customer needs, and selecting from a portfolio of solutions. Second, there's a revolution in information technologies that will have implications for prequalifying, internal support, and database marketing."

—Vice president, Scott Paper Company
(United States)

At the beginning of the chapter, we discussed the critical role that knowledge plays in helping the salesperson fulfill the role of business consultant and how customers expect salespeople to be more knowledgeable than ever before.

The bad news is that the knowledge base that salespeople need has expanded well beyond what any individual could possibly know. Salespeople need more information about products, services, customers, and competitors than ever before.

Often the need to gather and organize information lengthens the sales process. Also, the growing emphasis on team selling makes it critical to share information quickly and accurately among a wide variety of people who influence the account.

The good news is that technology has exploded the boundaries of today's knowledge frontiers: Salespeople have access to almost any conceivable piece of information or data.

Nearly every sales organization has invested in some sort of technology to automate certain steps in the sales process. In most cases, this technology helps salespeople use their precall time more efficiently, for example, to access information about the client. But many companies are looking for ways to use technology to improve salespeople's performance when they're *with* clients.

A new application of computer technologies, collectively known as electronic performance support systems (EPSS), is making this possible. Also referred to as integrated performance support systems (IPSS), an EPSS may be a shell program that accesses various information databases and links and organizes them with a minimum of effort on the part of the salesperson. An EPSS can often save the salesperson from having to interrupt the flow of a sales call to return to the office and gather information. It does this by allowing the salesperson to call up the information necessary on his or her computer almost instantly to make recommendations and assist the customer in making decisions *during* a sales call.

An example of an EPSS can be found at Intel Corporation (United States), which provides its 1000 sales representatives with what it calls the "I Know" performance support system. Developed by Ariel Corporation (United States), the system is accessed on the rep's notebook computer during a sales call and lets the sales rep:

- Compare two Intel products side by side.
- Compare Intel products against a competitive product.
- Develop "if/then" sales scenarios with recommended answers.
- Create custom presentations.

The EPSS provides Intel salespeople with the means to keep up with information about new products and to get the information they need, when they need it. It also decreases the time they spend on fact-finding and improves customer responsiveness.

Information technology has also been used by American Airlines (United States) to add value on sales calls—and to create a competitive advantage. American Airlines has made a major investment in information technology to analyze the factors that influence its own profitability and that of the travel agencies that book its flights. The data, downloaded onto each sales rep's notebook PC every month, are used on sales calls with travel agents. The salesperson can show the agents the increase in American Airlines bookings and the effect on their agency's commissions and overall market share.

Until recently, that information was available only if travel agencies gathered it themselves. When another airline announced its intention to provide similar information, American Airlines offered theirs in an updated form and at more frequent intervals. By adding value through unique information, salespeople at American Airlines bring themselves into closer partnership with customers while simultaneously building their company's share of its markets.

No matter which EPSS a company installs, however, it should be introduced in a logical fashion. Linsalata and Highland describe five common phases of a sales information system implementation, each one characterized by an increase in the amount of information shared with the customer:[1]

1. *Focus on providing the sales force with seamless communications and easy, convenient access to information.* During this stage, it is important to understand the company's strategy, as well as customers' needs, and to focus on identifying the information requirements of the customer and the sales process. Avoid the traditional systems engineering focus of automating existing manual procedures.

2. *Provide decision-support tools to leverage the newly available information.* An example would be a rules-based system that makes sales recommendations.

3. *Optimize the use of these technologies by reengineering the sales force to assume greater decision-making authority* and manage a broader range of products and customers. This involves releasing increasing amounts of information, responsibility, and authority from corporate headquarters to the sales organization.

4. *Integrate the customer's information systems to transfer some time-consuming tasks to the customer.* Some examples might be

---

[1]Ralph Linsalata and Richard Highland, "Reengineering the Selling Process," White Paper published by Eavoiy Systems Corporation, Waltham, MA.

preliminary price quotes, product availability, order entry, and new product introductions. With more time available, the sales rep can work with the customer on value-added projects and proposals.

5. *Review and refine the process to improve the customer-supplier relationship.* During this stage, it may be necessary to enhance the sales information system to support new customer requirements.

In addition, EPSSs have advantages outside the sales arena. For example, their ability to merge databases gives suppliers greater ability to capture and analyze information on how their customers buy products. This information can then be shared with the customer to permit more informed purchasing decisions. It can also be shared with the sales organization to make informed decisions about the marketplace.

In short, EPSS can dramatically increase the flexibility and responsiveness of a salesperson on a call, whereas traditional sales force technologies focus primarily on reducing costs by automating mechanical, repetitive processes (see comparison in Table 7-1).

CONCLUSION

The credibility of the salesperson is a critical factor in developing relationships with customers. Today, credibility is built by demonstrating comprehensive knowledge, outstanding communication skills, and the proper attitude. In this way, salespeople can fulfill the new role of business consultant.

BEST PRACTICES AND GUIDING PRINCIPLES

- From the start, salespeople have to build credibility by demonstrating general business knowledge and asking insightful questions—for instance, questions that get customers to think about issues and opportunities of which they may not have been aware. Knowledge can be demonstrated by discussing the customer's big-picture challenges and bottom-line realities, as well as what the customer has to do to personally succeed.

TABLE 7–1

Potential Impact of Electronic Performance Support Systems on a Sales Cycle

Factor	Without EPSS	With EPSS
Level of product knowledge the salesperson needs	Specific knowledge of all key products the company and competitors offer.	General knowledge of relevant company and competitive products, since the EPSS provides detailed information.
Where information exists	Primarily in databases and catalogues.	In connected databases.
How information can be accessed and organized	Salesperson or assistant locates and organizes information. This requires considerable backstage work.	Salesperson or customer uses EPSS to access and organize information instantly. Minimal backstage work is required.
Length of sales cycle	Longer, since sales calls are often terminated when further information is needed.	Shorter, since much more information is available during sales calls.

- Encourage your salespeople to take on the role of business consultant through the following practices:
  - Use contacts to acquire information about a customer's business.
  - Seek customers' and colleagues' perceptions of market trends, company direction, and potential product/service needs.
  - Find out what customers must do to succeed in their jobs.
  - Identify issues and needs at all levels (e.g., overriding business issues, organizational issues and priorities, functional and individual issues or needs).
  - Find or develop online or offline databases containing information on customers, industries, and the customers' own customers.

- Confirm understanding of each customer's mission, goals, strategies, markets, products/services, business functions, and competitors.
- Familiarize customers with your industry or company.
- Read newspapers, magazines, business journals, trade publications, and annual reports; attend conferences to increase knowledge of business and industries.
- Demonstrate the cost-cutting or revenue-producing benefits of products and services.
- Share useful business information with customers, even when it doesn't directly further the sales effort. Speak at listeners' levels of knowledge and sophistication. Use stories and analogies effectively.
- Seek feedback from customers on the clarity of communications.
- Acknowledge gaps in understanding or knowledge.
- Develop solutions in which the customer, supplier organization, and salespeople all "win."
- Never stop exploring ways to put relevant, up-to-date information into the salesperson's hands on a "just-in-time" basis. This will allow salespeople to focus more on the problem and the customer rather than on technical details of products, services, and solutions.

Chapter Eight

Salesperson as Long-Term Ally

"Sales activities continue long after you have sold the product. The objective is not only to get the sale, but to have customers use the product after buying it. That's why post-sale and follow-up are true sales activities. They are the key to profits and repeat orders."

—Sales representative, Fuji Xerox Company
(Japan)

- What do customers value in long-term relationships?
- How are alliances built?
- What is meant by the relationship gap?
- How can the relationship gap be closed?

Chapter Five discussed consultative selling as a critical strategy for many of the world's leading sales organizations. It enables them to develop the rapport, trust, and respect needed to strengthen customer relationships and gain competitive advantage. Chapters Five and Six examined the roles that strategic orchestrators and business consultants play in effective selling. This chapter examines the third role of consultative selling: long-term ally. Figure 8-1 again demonstrates the three roles of the salesperson.

FIGURE 8-1
Three Roles of the Consultative Salesperson

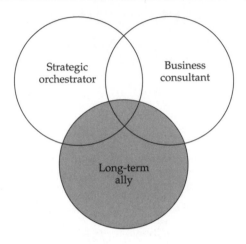

CUSTOMER'S PERSPECTIVE
ON LONG-TERM ALLIANCES

"The salesperson helps me look good in my organization and offers so-lutions where we both profit."

—Customer, Boehme
(Germany)

Sometimes, less is more. A study of Fortune 1000 companies, conducted by the National Association of Purchasing Management,[1] reveals the 10 most important trends that will influence purchasing decisions in the future. As Table 8-1 shows, purchasing managers ranked *reducing* the number of suppliers they work with as the single most important change in the way they work with suppliers. In addition, those surveyed agree that this change will also be the most important trend in the future, extending into the twenty-first century.

[1]As described in *Personal Selling Power* magazine (September 1993). Barry Retchfeld, *Personal Selling Power*, 13, no. 6, pp. 26–33.

TABLE 8-1
Purchasing Trends Ranked in Order of Importance

Current	Future	Trend
1	1	Fewer sources of supply will be used.
3	2	Customer satisfaction will count more for purchases.
2	3	Purchasers will manage supplier relations.
4	4	Purchasers will aim for shorter cycle times.
6	5	Supply chain management will receive greater emphasis.
7	6	Engineers and buyers will work together as a team.
8	7	Purchasers will buy more from foreign producers.
10	8	Ordering will be more decentralized.
9	9	Teams will choose suppliers.
5	10	Single sourcing will increase.

There are many reasons why customers want to work with fewer suppliers:

- Because the demands of their own customers change rapidly, buyers do not have the time to constantly experiment with or "break in" a new supplier. They must limit the number of supplier organizations with which they work. The organizations they choose to work with must be able to provide reliable, flexible support before, during, and after the sale.

- In addition, the decisions customers make today are much more complex and more likely to have a direct impact on the company's strategic direction than ever before.[2]

- As a result, customers expect to work with salespeople and supplier organizations who understand their strategies and can develop solutions to a wide range of immediate and long-term needs. They expect to work with salespeople who can fulfill the roles of strategic orchestrator, business consultant, and long-term ally throughout the business relationship.

---

[2]For more information, see Chapter Two.

Associated Spring: Building Long-Term Relationships with Suppliers[3]

Theresa Metty, director of materials for Associated Spring, part of the Barnes Group in Bristol, Connecticut (United States), has headed up the development of a comprehensive supplier relations program that has cut the number of suppliers by more than half.

"We are interested in building much longer-term relationships now than in past years," Metty says. "We used to have suppliers who were in and out and then back again. Now, once in, they stay in as long as they can perform. Instead of having several suppliers for a given commodity, we now have perhaps two. That's as low as we can go without endangering continuity of supply."

The advantage, says Metty, is that her company knows it can count on those two suppliers, and they know they can count on Associated Spring. If a supplier has problems, Associated Spring will work with the supplier intensively rather than shutting it off as it used to.

The implication for sales organizations is clear. Any sales organization that hopes to meet these customer expectations must have salespeople who are able to position themselves and the company as a *long-term ally.* Personnel at top-performing sales organizations around the world say that developing long-term relationships with customers will be absolutely critical to the success of their business.

BUILDING ALLIANCES

"Salespeople must constantly keep track of each customer's situation, how it has changed, and what the customer wants to do about it. They can't assume the customer's situation is stable or that its needs stay the same."

—Salesperson, Northwestern Mutual Life Insurance Company
(United States)

What can salespeople do to put themselves and their organizations on the road to long-term alliances with their customers? Research

---

[3]James S. Howard, "Suppliers and Customers Put Down the Gloves," *D & B Reports 41*, no. 3 (May/June 1992), pp. 26–28.

identified 20 practices that characterize successful long-term allies, based upon surveys completed by 650 salespeople and 155 sales managers in 13 companies throughout North America. The best salespeople actively display a long-term perspective of the relationship and a commitment to their customers' future. They do this by continually looking for ways to:

- Build interpersonal trust.
- Create and sustain a positive image of the sales organization.
- Inspire respect for their company.
- Demonstrate concern for their customers' long-term, as well as immediate, interests.
- Identify ways to strengthen the quality of their business relationships.
- Help the customer meet needs within his or her organization.
- Resolve issues openly and honestly.
- Deliver on promises.

Another critical activity for the salesperson is to ensure that the relationship between the two organizations is mutually beneficial. At the heart of the concept of being long-term allies is an expectation that the agreements will be good business for both organizations.

Sales managers across all industries have strong opinions about the need to develop a balance, or a sense of fairness and equity, in the partnership between the buyer and seller organizations. This is a marked difference in attitude since Learning International's customer service research was conducted several years ago. At that time, supplier organizations said that they were "adding value" by offering the customer more at lower cost. Today, organizations are more sophisticated about the need to maintain profitability *and* achieve customer satisfaction and the importance of making trade-offs to achieve both goals in the long run.

Long-Term Ally

A salesperson who demonstrates commitment—and is able to contribute—to the customer's short- and long-term success throughout the entire Customer Relationship Process.

In a British research study, Eugene Fram and Martin Presberg interviewed 133 sales managers to examine supplier experiences with purchasing partners. Many lamented the inordinate burden suppliers must bear in maintaining mutually profitable relationships. Over time, said the managers, customers typically ask for the most costly services, "cherry pick" low-margin items to the detriment of the supplier, or withhold information on needs and goals. In most cases, it's up to the supplier to resolve these strains or find solutions both parties can live with. [4]

What does a successful alliance entail? While every alliance is different, the ones we studied have several characteristics in common. They are summarized in Table 8-2.

One organization that is committed to developing long-term relationships is Xerox Corporation (United States). Acting as long-term allies to their customers, Xerox sales professionals cultivate

TABLE 8–2
Long-Term Allies and Mutually Beneficial Agreements

Supplier organization must be willing to . . .	*Buyer organization must be willing to . . .*
Solicit feedback from customers regarding overall satisfaction with the products/services delivered	Keep suppliers "in the loop" regarding the company's strategic direction and needs
Maintain regular contact with current and prospective customers	Value the record of service provided by supplier organization above lower-cost competitors
Alert customers to new developments in own organization	Grant access and information about their customers to the supplier organization
Review the business relationship underlying each account regularly	

---

[4] Reported in the *Journal of Business and Industrial Marketing 8,* no. 4 (1993).

relationships by building trust, researching options, and offering recommendations designed to solve the customer's strategic business problems.

Xerox believes the partnership role will be increasingly significant in helping companies survive global competition during the next decade. This sales approach is delivering more profits to Xerox than the "make a sale at any cost" approach of the past.

In the European food industry, leading suppliers such as Unilever and Procter & Gamble are developing partnerships with their key customers. These partnerships go well beyond traditional buyer/seller relationships. They involve all aspects of the organization, including the links between account managers and category managers, between the logistics operations of both sides, between accounts outgoing and receiving. Electronic Data Interchange (EDI) is one element of how these organizations achieve major savings through closer relationships.

To develop a successful alliance, salespeople must focus on the customers' customers. Ultimately, the customers' success is based on their ability to meet and exceed their own customers' expectations. A salesperson's success will largely depend on how well he or she helps them do that.

"What's unique about Scott," said one distributor of Scott Paper Company (United States), "is that they don't think of the distributor as the ultimate customer. We work in partnership with them to reach the end user. They always keep in mind that the end user is the ultimate customer. This is different from most of their competitors who think of the distributor as the ultimate customer. Scott really understands the idea of partnership and they really believe it."

CLOSING THE RELATIONSHIP GAP

"In a competitive society, the customer's demands are, in a sense, absolute. We commit ourselves to meeting the customer's expectations and building a trustworthy relationship."

—Senior general manager of component marketing group,
Sony Corporation
(Japan)

The ability of a salesperson to fulfill the role of long-term ally is a pivotal factor in determining whether a sales interaction is just a *transaction* or the beginning of a relationship. The focus on long-term relationships is a dramatic change from the way sales organizations, and salespeople, have traditionally defined their roles. As shown in Figure 8-2, many salespeople have considered their roles fulfilled when the sale is made. However, there is a tremendous opportunity to develop a long-term relationship by fulfilling the role of the long-term ally long *after* the sale.

FIGURE 8-2
Managing the Relationship Gap

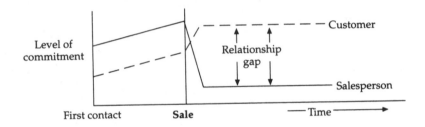

Partners and Long-Term Allies

When it comes to describing the desired, long-term state of affairs between customers and sales organizations, many different terms are used interchangeably. The most common ones used today are "partnership" and relationship."

The term *partnership* often describes a comprehensive and strategic relationship between two organizations—one in which the two companies have made a formal commitment to work together to achieve a shared objective. In some cases, the companies may even agree to change their business processes to accommodate each other.

The ability of a salesperson to fulfill the role of long-term ally is critical to the success of partnerships and long-term business relationships.

Figure 8-2 shows a typical relationship between a buyer and seller over time. Initially, the customer's level of commitment to the process is low, and the supplier's level of commitment is high. After the sale, the salesperson's interest in dealing with the customer's concerns often drops substantially.

Conversely, after the sale, the customer's interest in the success of the implementation increases rapidly. The vast difference between the customer's and the salesperson's post-sale levels of concern has been referred to as the *relationship gap*.

Salespeople who fulfill the role of long-term ally work to eliminate the relationship gap by ensuring that the customer is receiving the level of support and service that meets his or her expectation now *and* throughout the duration of the Customer Relationship Process.

CONCLUSION

The limited resources that all companies face in today's business environment are driving the need to build stronger bonds between suppliers and customers and to develop long-term relationships.

Salespeople who are able to position themselves as long-term allies earn the right to be one of the customer's long-term suppliers. In so doing, they help their companies stand out in the marketplace and contribute to their growth and prosperity.

BEST PRACTICES AND GUIDING PRINCIPLES

- Encourage your salespeople to take on the role of long-term ally through the following practices:
  - Identify opportunities to make personal commitments and keep the commitments they make.
  - Seize opportunities to convey pride and confidence in the products/services and respect for the way the company operates.
  - Fully educate prospective users about product features, benefits, and applications.
  - Educate customers about a competitor's products/services (when appropriate).

- Respond thoroughly and honestly to customer concerns.
- Position the capabilities and shortcomings of your products and organization realistically, and highlight the positives of your own products and organization instead of the negatives of your competitors' products or organizations.
- Make recommendations on the basis of customers' long-term needs, not on what the salesperson needs to sell.
- Turn down business not in the customers' long-term interests.
- "Go to bat" for customers within your company.
- Negotiate contracts in which customers *and* one's own company win in the long run.
- Regularly assert availability and desire to be of service.
- Identify ways to make customers look good in the eyes of their own colleagues and superiors.
- Help customers carry out fact-finding or "selling" strategies within their own company.
- Elicit information from customers that helps them define and strengthen the direction of future business.
- Maintain contact with customers even when there's no prospect of an immediate sale.
- Foster mutual respect by asking for—as well as providing—assistance, information, and honesty.
- Identify information and services that salespeople could provide that would be valuable to customers.
- "Go the extra mile" whenever necessary—for instance, help customers carry out fact-finding missions.

III

CRITICAL SUCCESS FACTORS

"The salesperson is the ambassador of the company."

Chapter Nine

Technology-Enabled Selling: Wiring the Enterprise for High-Performance Selling

"The next information revolution is forcing us to redefine what business enterprise actually is—the creation of value and wealth."

—Peter F. Drucker

- A day in the life of the technology-enabled sales team
- Technology tools: past, present, and future
- The Internet

Pop quiz! Test your techno-savvy by matching the word or acronym with its functional definition. (The answers are on page 107.)

1. Smaller than a hand-held PC, it's a digital way to take notes, schedule appointments, or look up customers' phone numbers. _____   a) ERP

2. The largest TCP/IP network in the world. _____   b) Intranet

3. Combines phone and computer technologies. _____   c) SFA/CRM

4. Customers use it to execute simple tasks or requests through a touch-tone phone or by voice recognition. _____   d) Knowledge Management

5. Slice and dice data to find the hidden trends. _____   e) Sales Configurator

6. A thorough collection of all marketing and sales materials that salespeople can use to create customized presentations. _____   f) Internet

7. Kinder, gentler reengineering, it integrates human insight about work processes with computer processing power to measure results and provide feedback. _____   g) Marketing Encyclopedia

8. A private Internet for your organization. _____   h) CTI

9. Computer application designed to support sales activities, such as scheduling and contact management. _____   i) IVR

10. The information backbone of the enterprise. _____   j) PDA

11. Lets salespeople compare options and pricing for customers. _____   k) Data Mining

How did you do?[1] If some of those terms were unfamiliar to you, no need to worry: Technology is advancing at such a fast pace that it's virtually impossible to keep up. And if you scored 100 percent, don't grow too smug: New terms are being added to the technology lexicon almost as fast as new Websites are appearing on the Internet! Fortunately, even in a world dominated by Internet-time and its imperatives, the present and the future still build on the past. Our goal in this chapter is to talk about what technology solutions work now and what strategies and solutions will continue to work in the future.

THE TECHNOLOGY IMPERATIVE: A DAY IN THE LIFE. . .

The technology question that any top-performing sales organization is asking focuses not on "Should we . . .?" but on "How can we . . .?"

More importantly: "How can we . . . better and faster than our competitors?"

Top-performing sales organizations properly implement and use *the most appropriate technology* to sell and serve customers more effectively than competitors. For them, many of the terms in the quiz are not static concepts. They identify the vital organs, muscle, bone, and sinew that connect all the parts of the company so its resources are at the fingertips of the person interacting with the customer. We'll see that technology can transform the strategic orchestrator role by providing a salesperson with an enhanced understanding of, and access to, the many different value components needed to win current business and *add ongoing value in an account.* What follows is a possible scenario:

> *This feels so good,* thought Laura Webber as she and a few hundred other salespeople exited the conference room doors. Squeezing through the crowd around the coffee stations, she picked up speed and strode down the hallway toward the front lobby of the hotel. After sitting all morning listening to presentations, the simple act of walking was a pleasure.
>
> As field sales manager at Standard Office, a successful Midwestern office products manufacturer, Laura had been concerned about leaving the office for even a few days, as Standard Office was feeling increased pressure from value-priced competitors.

---

[1]Answers: to quiz on preceding page: 1-j; 2-f; 3-h; 4-I; 5-k; 6-g; 7-d; 8-b; 9-c; 10-a; 11-e.

The two-day sales and marketing conference was nearly over. She had picked up some solid ideas about electronic commerce, as well as reward-and-recognition programs that had cut sales rep turnover for other managers. During this break, she figured she had just enough time to step outside for a breath of fresh air, then find a chair and check e-mail. All in all, she felt pretty good. That would all change with a few mouse clicks.

Scott Johnson, the new purchasing director at one of Standard's biggest customers, Better Care Health Systems, was viewing the Web-site of Value Office, one of the cut-rate interlopers in Laura's market.

Scott was looking for ways to cut costs. He had learned that Better Care, a large HMO, bought most of their office equipment from Standard. He also had noticed that his chair and his coworkers' chairs were better than those at his former job.

"Maybe it's time for a change," Scott thought, adjusting his arm rests higher as he viewed the competition's offerings. From what he had seen so far, it appeared that Value Office's furniture would be just fine for equipping the big new West Coast office—and it would cost substantially less than Standard's. He clicked on an e-mail link and requested some brochures. Then he surfed to Standard's Website for some comparison shopping.

"I really don't see much difference," Scott thought. "All right, their steel is heavier gauge and the air cylinders on the chairs are heavy duty, but it's just office furniture. We're not launching people into outer space."

Noticing that Standard's site had a "help" button, Scott clicked on it with his mouse. CTI software at Standard's Midwest Call Center recognized the call as coming from a key customer.

In keeping with Standard's Customer Relationship Management (CRM) philosophy, the system enables Standard to identify and segment customers. It routs calls from smaller customers to an interactive voice response (IVR) application prompting them to choose from a menu: speak to a call center agent, place an order, or enter the first few digits of a product code to be connected with an agent with expertise about that line. Dealers are switched to senior agents with broad product knowledge and experience.

Large clients, including Better Care, are routed to teams of specially trained inside salespeople assigned to that customer.

As it identified Scott's inbound call, the CTI system accessed an account database. The account information arrived at the salesperson's computer as a "screen pop," synchronized to be displayed as the call arrived at the headset. This eliminated the need for the customer to repeat information to a series of agents before being connected with the right person. It dovetailed nicely with Standard's emphasis on service to distinguish it from the cut-rate crowd.

When the screen pop arrived with Scott's call, salesperson David Jones noticed a recent entry from Laura about her efforts to set up a meeting with Scott to discuss equipment purchases for the new office.

"I'm looking at your Website," Scott said to David. "I was just at Value Office's site and to be honest, it looks like they have good quality products at much better prices than yours."

"What Web page are you looking at?" asked David. With Standard's new Web-enabled interactive customer contact application, he was able to view the same page as Scott. The application also provided text fields and page markup features that allow a customer and sales rep to type messages in a chat box or use the mouse to mark pages. The customer can see what the agent marks or writes and vice versa. It also lets an agent "push" Web pages to customers for viewing.

"Let's look at some of the unique benefits of our equipment," said David, "pushing" Scott a Web page that described an ergonomic chair. Using his mouse, David circled the air cylinder at the base of the chair. "That's a higher-quality, heavier-duty unit than Value Office offers," he said. "Our chairs last a lot longer, and that lowers your life-cycle costs. The height adjustment stays where it is set, which means your people always work at the most comfortable position. And that helps you control stress-related disabilities."

"I don't know," said Scott. "I can't believe it makes that much difference, especially at the price you're asking. I'm supposed to meet with Laura Webber next week, but to tell you the truth, I don't know if it's going to be necessary. Well, thanks for the information. I'll take a look at these Web pages you sent and get back to you."

Feeling a big customer slipping away, David sent an urgent e-mail to Laura.

Laura found a chair near a lobby window. She pulled out her hand-held PC and connected it to the wireless modem. The company had purchased the equipment for her and her field salespeople when the new functionality was added to the Website. It was all part of a continuing effort to provide better service than their cut-rate competitors.

In the past, Laura had used voice mail to keep in touch with the office and her reps. Voicemail required always being on the lookout for public phones or private areas to use her cellular phone. And many people check e-mail only once or twice a day because of the hassle of hooking up bulky notebook computers.

With her new hand-held unit, wireless modem and wireless Internet service provider, Laura can access the Internet, send e-mails, get stock updates or news from the company intranet, run a spreadsheet or word-processing applications, or work on a proposal and zap it back to her boss for review.

This way, at any short meeting break she can "fire up" the modem and computer. Laura was definitely checking her e-mail more frequently. More importantly, her salespeople loved them. Since it is easier to stay in touch and she quickly responds to their messages, they're more willing to keep her and other managers in the loop with short e-mails.

Laura and the other managers have found that the new computers were helping them all maintain peace of mind. No more piles of questions on their desks or in their e-mail inboxes when they returned from trips.

Scanning her e-mail inbox during this conference break, Laura noticed the "urgent" message from David. It sounded as though Scott was getting ready to let the competition furnish the new offices. She called David on her cell phone. She asked him to begin gathering material from Standard's Marketing Encyclopedia and the company's intranet—including the new video of a presentation by the head of engineering on ergonomics. Armed with this information, the new presentation software, and its intelligent SalesAid expert system, she could put together a customized presentation and have it ready to show Scott the next afternoon.

In fact, Laura would be in Scott's office, showing him the customized presentation before the brochures from Value Office were even in the mail. By the time they arrived, she planned to be in Scott's office with a proposal on his desk.

SALES FORCE AUTOMATION AND CUSTOMER RELATIONSHIP MANAGEMENT SOFTWARE

As this fictional story illustrates, rapid advances in computer technology have spawned software systems that are changing the face of sales and marketing while increasing productivity and cutting costs. Leading the way are a host of Sales Force Automation (SFA) and Customer Relationship Management (CRM) software applications.

The marketplace for those applications, and their functionality, is evolving rapidly. The change in software category name (moving more toward CRM) is indicative of a change in focus for marketing those tools: how they are used by salespeople and how the sales organization values its salespeople and its customers. It's a positive trend. No one really believes that a sales force of automatons (SFA) is what senior management is after, and what better way to win in the marketplace than using tools that put customer needs and the customer relationship (CRM) at the center of the sales enterprise?

Automating sales and marketing is certainly not a new concept. In the early days, people did it by running VisiCalc on Apple IIs. Later, software developers began releasing SFA software. Although it was difficult to use and didn't successfully model business practices, it captured the minds and wallets of sales organizations willing to learn at the "bleeding edge." Today, fortunately, new advancements have led to software that is more closely targeted to the salesperson's needs, the sales organization's automation objectives, and rising customer expectations for a professional business relationship.

In general, high-performance organizations that implemented SFA and CRM successfully did so by keeping two objectives clearly in mind:

1. Reduce the cost of finding and closing deals with new customers, thus increasing overall profit.
2. Retain customers by ensuring that they have positive experiences in *all* aspects of the sale—and beyond.

Implemented effectively, SFA/CRM can enable and emphasize enterprisewide information sharing, provide customer information that is the bedrock of almost supernatural customer support, and deliver real competitive advantage. It also can help salespeople sell in a more consultative—and, therefore, effective—manner by supplying and enabling the easy use of high-yield sales probing strategies and questions that uncover customer needs and identify opportunities.

Studies of successful implementations also indicate additional benefits: a reduction in sales force turnover and an increase in revenue per person. By helping salespeople succeed, it appears SFA/CRM can help differentiate an organization from its competitors—both on the sales front and in the effort to recruit and retain top performers. And as we know from our 1999 survey of sales managers and VPs, there is no issue more pressing than recruiting and retaining quality salespeople.

The Long and Winding Road

The road to a successful sales automation implementation has never been an easy one to navigate. The SFA/CRM world has been

criticized for its high rate of failure and its high cost of implementation. But as the market has matured, organizations have learned
that success is probably as dependent on implementation planning
and execution as it is on software selection. Once in use, systems
rise and fall based on how well they address a clear business challenge. Great software *requires* enthusiastic users to realize its value.
Making that happen requires a rock-solid strategy from the top
down. In a sales organization that builds positive user expectations,
these expectations must be based on clearly articulated group and
individual benefits of using the new technology.

Every end user must know the answer to the WIIFM (What's In
It For Me?) question even before using any new productivity tool.
Ignoring the WIIFM factor can stop an SFA/CRM initiative faster
than you can boot up your Palm Pilot™. Early SFA software was designed to help individual salespeople with contact management. It
was essentially an automated appointment and address book. The
current generation of SFA tools, now often referred to as Customer
Relationship Management (CRM) software, offers more robust
functionality, often designed for work groups and featuring more
sophisticated project management capabilities. Such software can:

- Assess the profit margin for every sales project.
- Help managers analyze why some deals are more profitable
  than others.
- Improve the working relationship between regional sales offices
  by frequently updating and synchronizing the database shared
  by both offices.

Fully functional SFA/CRM software integrates financial, manufacturing, and marketing information, letting an enterprise install a
single system to manage all aspects of sales, marketing, and customer service. The best packages manage accounts, contacts, leads,
and products, and help you find product and market information
via the Internet or on your corporate intranet.

When integrating SFA/CRM applications across the enterprise,
two key items are often left out of the planning process—putting the
entire undertaking at risk:

Customer needs

The real impact occurs when the company matches the sales cycle to
the purchasing cycle and to the clients' needs. If you look at

SFA/CRM as an isolated technology deployment instead of part of an overall reengineering or refocusing effort designed to enhance customer satisfaction, the project's payoff won't live up to expectations.

The quality of the sales process itself

SFA/CRM, like most technology today, enables people to get more things accomplished. But that in itself is no guarantee that what is getting done is providing any value to anyone. Most sales directors would salivate at the prospect of software that would help their salespeople double the number of sales calls they could make in a day. But if the sales skills and processes the salesperson uses are ineffective to begin with, all you've done is spend a lot of money to automate a mediocre performance model. It's our old friend (or nemesis?) "better, faster, cheaper" without the "better" part. Faster and cheaper are the cornerstones of the commodity marketplace. Better is what separates you from the pack and enables pricing based on the customer's expectation and perception of real value solutions.

ROTI: Return on Technology Investment

Mary Committee, president of Atlanta-based Marketing Mastery, is a strong believer in the power of technology-enabled sales to make the investment pay off. But she notes that to achieve an acceptable ROI, successful companies must go after increased effectiveness as opposed to increased volume of sales calls. In other words, while salespeople may make the same number of calls, the system helps them target better customer candidates, more fully understand customer needs, and shorten sales cycles. Committee offers the following guidelines to developing an effective technology ROI:

- Understand the company's top five corporate objectives.
- Determine the most valuable applications.
- Develop an ROI model with hard dollar values.
- Keep it simple.

As an example, Committee cites a temporary service company that aimed to reduce turnover rate in its sales staff, increase repeat business from customers, continue earnings growth, and increase customer satisfaction. Realizing that high sales-force turnover was in the nature of its business, the company embraced the turnover rates as a positive thing because it kept the sales force fresh.

It addressed the issue by installing an SFA/CRM system. Now new salespeople have customer histories on hand and are prompted to follow up on active accounts with news of promotions. The system sponsors first estimated conservatively that this would help increase each new salesperson's effectiveness by 5 percent, from $200,000 per year to $210,000 in sales, which translated to a $1.3 million total increase per year.

"The actual number turned out to be much higher," Committee says.[2]

Potential Pitfalls

Although the potential benefits to businesses are huge, automation of any kind will fail without careful implementation. Last year, the Gartner Group estimated that 60 to 65 percent of all SFA/CRM projects fail to produce measurable benefits.[3] The potential benefits and costs of these systems are too high to tolerate such a high rate of failure.

Failure doesn't often occur at the beginning of a project, but from neglect along the way. As Fore Systems, Inc., learned, SFA/CRM projects are doomed unless they are part of an *ongoing* overall organizational effort.[4]

Beyond Gartner's failure data for last year, most analysts agree that more than 50 percent of SFA/CRM projects fail or at least fall far short of expectations. Key among the reasons for the low success rate is the difficulty of getting buy-in from the salespeople who often view the technology and the time required to learn and use it as a hindrance instead of a help.

Other common hurdles are cultural issues that divide the information technology (IS) community from the sales force and encourage resistance including the inability to roll out new technology effectively, and building SFA/CRM systems in isolation from other back-office automation projects, such as ERP (enterprise resource planning) deployments.

Even if the sales force does leap on the bandwagon, that in itself doesn't ensure success—especially if the project doesn't tie in with the rest of the organization.

---

[2]*InfoWorld* (Aug. 31, 1998).
[3]*Sales & Marketing Management,* May 1997.
[4]*PC Week* (June 15, 1998).

The Bottom Line

Many companies are just beginning to go "full speed ahead" with technology-enabled selling of one kind or another, while others have used some kind of technology for decades. Those that dive in now may find the price tag high, but it's often more expensive if you don't automate. Fully implemented, SFA/CRM can cost up to $1 million for a high-end application. Add to this initial investment in software the network costs, training, and ongoing support, and the price appears monumental. Current estimates for a full CRM implementation are over $10,000 per salesperson. But you can measure the return on investment (ROI) in more than dollars alone, as the following example (featured in *InfoWorld*, Aug. 31, 1998) illustrates:

> The Endeavor Group, in Newport Beach, California, provides annuities to brokers, insurance agents, and independent financial planners. The company expects to see sales rise 10 percent to 12 percent once it gets its sales and marketing package, Moss Micro's ActiveSales, set up in early September, according to V. J. McGuinness, Endeavor's chief operations officer.
>
> "I think this will help us capture more market share and get on more [sellers'] preferred lists," McGuinness says. "I'm hoping this will be a 'killer app' in our business."
>
> McGuinness explains that it is hard for companies such as Endeavor to tally sales directly because they only make annuities—secure, long-term investments—available to retail financial planners, who then sell the annuities directly to the consumers (who usually buy them to pay for retirement or support survivors).
>
> That means Endeavor measures salespeople's outcome not by the number of annuities they sell but the number of sales and service calls they make to retail providers, teaching them the features of each product and advising them on how to market them. Also, Endeavor salespeople may be brought in to pitch the annuities directly to a prospective audience, such as workers eligible for their company's 401(k) plan, McGuinness says.
>
> Tracking those account calls has been time-consuming and costly. Endeavor's staff currently uses several different software programs, including several separate databases, a couple of contact management programs, Microsoft Outlook, Microsoft Office, and e-mail, McGuinness says. Field salespeople fill out weekly call reports, which they then photocopy and fax or deliver to the home office, where two data-entry clerks work full-time just inputting them.

But once the field force gets up to speed on ActiveSales, they will send in their reports electronically, saving $20,000 to $30,000 per year on copying and mailing costs and freeing up at least half of each day for the data-entry clerks to do more productive things, McGuinness says.

Moreover, the ease of sharing data electronically should lead to more up-to-date and therefore more valuable files of current and prospective contacts, McGuinness says. This will help the sales staff boost the bottom line by concentrating on the most valuable accounts, while lowering marketing costs by cutting mailings to invalid addresses.

Roadmap for SFA/CRM Success

For a successful automation project, you need to take the following steps:[5]

- Involve the users in every stage of the process. Seeking input from users empowers them to develop a system they will use. If they don't want it, don't understand it, or can't use it, it's doomed from the start. Assigning a successful and respected field salesperson as an internal consultant from the start of the project can help ensure inclusion of the "voice of the field" and jump-start acceptance once the system is in production ("computerese" for out of testing and actually being used).

- Get upper-level managers to commit to the project. Without this commitment and some well-publicized on-going involvement, the project will never get off the ground.

- Analyze current business processes and change those that need changing. Managers who do their homework implement the most successful SFA/CRM/CM systems. They understand what they need to automate, and they involve the users and at times customers from the beginning.

- Select software based on realistic corporate needs. Users should be involved in software selection. If the software isn't easy to use with an understandable interface or if it's inflexible, the users won't use it to its potential.

- Train, train, train! Although training can be expensive (Goldenberg estimates up to three times the entire cost of the system over its lifetime), it gives users the tools they need to use the system intelligently and efficiently.

---

[5]Anne Fischer Lent. *Automating the World of Business Sales & Marketing Management* (May 1997). P2A(4)

- Follow up on every aspect of the process to ensure that the system meets your needs. Constant follow-up and motivation helps users to join in the system's evolution, letting them identify the changes that they need and then see those changes implemented.

INTERNET: THE ULTIMATE SALES RESOURCE

What salesperson or sales manager is not using the Internet in some way? While using e-mail to stay in touch with customers or colleagues is the most common use, sales professionals at leading companies also use it to do research, gather leads, and participate in web-enabled sales training events.

For research, they visit competitors' Websites to get competitive information or use their favorite search engine to gather preselling background on a prospect or client. But the Web is fast becoming much more than an online library.

Companies are demanding Web functionality in SFA/CRM applications, which puts increased emphasis on Internet/intranet capabilities. Using the Web, businesses can now connect help desk, customer service, marketing, and other functions across the Internet.[6]

By enabling users to access information themselves, the Web helps lower IT (information technology) costs, boosts marketing efforts, and underpins Web-based support. Customers expect support 24 hours a day, 7 days a week (24–7), and the Web enables companies to provide it. Customers can look up FAQs (frequently asked questions) and technical literature, or access customer service on the Web. This "self-service" approach lets users feel more independent and self-sufficient, enhancing their satisfaction. At the same time, the Web allows companies to lower their support costs because they need fewer people to staff the call center.

Enhancing Internal Communications

The Web also enhances internal corporate communications. Using a Web browser, customers, marketing groups, and sales teams can all access the same information. This capability lets people seek solutions

---

[6]*Sales & Marketing Management* (see footnote #5) (May 1997).

on their own, while reducing the IT costs of supporting software for each group.

Customer Relationship Management (CRM) systems are using the Internet to let Website visitors submit a form that is routed to an appropriate salesperson and to the salesperson's manager.[7] It's not just an e-mail; it also goes into the database. More sophisticated Internet lead-processing systems automatically generate a literature fulfillment request and remind a salesperson to call the prospect immediately. After the sale, the system routes the order through accounting, issues an invoice, chronicles the order's history, and automatically generates a markup or profit margin report for the sales manager.

In the near future, more sales managers will add lead filtering, programming that sorts out junk Internet leads from the good ones coming in through the Websites.

Sales Information Databases

Software can also enable a Website to track the activity and personal preferences of individual net users and send out sales information to those users based on their preferences. *Selling Power* (Jan./Feb. 1999) reports that Bowne Internet Solutions of Cambridge, MA, already provides software to build an e-commerce site that grows wiser over time about the personality and habits of each individual visitor.

One of Bowne's highest profile sites is an arts and entertainment guide, eGenie, that does not require users to fill out excruciatingly long questionnaires before it can begin to analyze their interests through its patent-pending learning agent.

The agent embedded in a Website's software tracks the path each user makes through the eGenie Website and uses artificial intelligence and machine-learning techniques to learn about the visitor's preferences. The software then makes product suggestions based on that expanding knowledge.

---

[7]Joe Dysart, "Custom made: How to make CRN work better for your bottom line," *Selling Power* (Jan./Feb. 1999), pp 87–88.

In addition, eGenie's learning agent can adapt to a user's changing interests. A teenager regularly visiting eGenie who develops a yen for science fiction six months later, for example, will find that over time the Website will automatically begin to recommend more sci-fi entertainment products. But as Websites like this begin to proliferate on the Web, the battle over sales prospecting versus privacy rights is sure to flare up again.

A look at the highlights of eGenie's functionality is a peek at the sales cycle of the future. It uses an intelligent questioning technique to acquire information from a customer/prospect. Then it makes product recommendations based on knowledge gained from the customer and builds a more complete understanding of the customer's preferences over time.

Does this sound like part of a salesperson's traditional responsibility set? As technology improves (about as risky as proposing that the sun will rise tomorrow) automated selling engines like eGenie will give new meaning to Sales Force Automation. That shift will be a wholesale one. As a result, face-to-face salespeople will move out of the prospecting arena and compete for well-qualified business by building trust (business consultant), delivering solutions (strategic orchestrator), and maintaining customer-focused relationships (long-term ally).

Enhancing Customer Relationships and Sales Productivity

While most other companies are still using the Web primarily as a marketing tool, Cisco Systems is using the Web to grow its customer relationships via its site, Cisco Connection Online (www.cisco.com), which gets hundreds of thousands of hits a month. The Website is another tool in the sales force's arsenal. It allows customers to track the status of their orders and get pricing and availability information, freeing the salespeople at the San Jose, California-based networking products company to do what they do best—sell. And that has translated into both cost savings and new business. By early 1998, the Website was producing $9 million in sales a day—or $3 billion a year. That equals 50 percent of the company's total revenue. And while revenue grew 35 percent last year, Cisco's customer service organization grew only 10 percent. Using the Web to provide customer service has helped the company avoid hiring more than

1000 technical-support engineers in the past two years. It also frees Cisco's salespeople; instead of answering customers' questions about order status and technical problems, they can focus on maintaining existing relationships and finding new accounts.[8]

VIRTUAL SALES TOOLS

Other high-tech tools used by leading sales organizations to close deals and serve customers include:[9]

- *3-D presentations* let customers go beyond spec sheets and walk through a product presentation. Product and order errors are reduced because customers see exactly what a product will look like before it is built. Result: a shorter sales cycle and happier customers.

- *Virtual reality presentations* use animation and 3-D imagery to educate customers by showing them case studies in action, in contrast to catalogs or schematics.

- *Sales Configurators* allow salespeople to take a variety of specs and configure products, while providing pricing and identifying possible problems in production. For example, Campaign Management Software is designed to help marketers plan, execute, evaluate, and refine marketing programs. FedEx began using campaign management software to make the transition from a product-focused business model to a customer-focused one by closely tracking marketing programs and monitoring customer feedback to learn how the company can improve its service. Marketing executives at the company estimate that FedEx has seen an 8-to-1 return on its direct-marketing investments as a result. That includes reducing its direct-marketing campaign cycles from 26 weeks to 8; a 65 percent revenue gain for its First Overnight product; and a 284 percent improvement in its prospecting campaigns. What's more, the software now lets FedEx's nontechnical marketing professionals run complicated campaigns that were once the domain of

---

[8] Melanie Berger, "Net sales: Cisco Connection Online Website," *Sales & Marketing Management* (April 1998), pp 90–91.

[9] Lambeth Hochsald, "Simplify: high-tech solutions can make selling a complex product easy." *Sales & Marketing Management* (June 1998), pp 65–67.

programmers. The result has been higher customer satisfaction and a better understanding of the company's campaign results.

- *Wireless sales tools:* The wireless market for voice and data is one of the fastest-growing areas in telecommunications, according to market research firm Frost and Sullivan Inc. in Mountain View, California. Wireless revenue, which totaled $1.8 billion in 1989, grew to about $4.5 billion in 1995, thanks in part to the fast expanding mobile market. Wireless tools aid reps in such industries such as perishable goods, medical supplies, and building supplies where the sales force is moving high-volume product with a time-sensitive order-fulfillment crunch. Other industries benefiting from wireless sales forces include those where information is constantly changing. In the semiconductor industry, inventory is continually in flux and new products are added regularly. Consequently, field salespeople need to know what they can and cannot deliver while they're in front of customers. If a rep inks a deal and then later, back in the hotel room retrieving e-mail, learns that the product won't be available, the result could be a lost customer, not just a lost sale.

- *Alphanumeric pagers* enable salespeople to receive messages unobtrusively. Unlike a cell phone that rings and that the user must answer, or a wireless notebook that the rep has to fire up, alphanumeric pagers put the power in the hands of the salesperson. "If I'm with a client, I don't want my cell phone to start ringing, nor do I want to miss an important message," says one rep. "But if my pager starts vibrating, I can glance down at it and get that message or press a button to shut it off . It's my choice." Based on the traditional paging networks, the more advanced alphanumeric pagers can receive text messages in the range of 120 to 140 characters in length.

A FINAL NOTE

Technology offers endless opportunity for investment and temporary advantage to forward-thinking sales organizations. It's only a temporary advantage because very little technology is proprietary. The benefits provided by a technology investment can and will be copied by competitors. Technology investments will always be necessary, but they are truly table stakes. Winning will require what it has always required: solid linkage between organization and sales strategy, a sales organization focused around the customer, and sales teams and individual salespeople able to deliver the entire organizational portrait of value in support of customer needs.

DEFINITIONS

CD-ROM business card. The size of a credit card, these can be printed with typical business information, but they also store information in any combination of text, graphics, photos, audio, video, documents, spreadsheets, presentations, and links to e-mail or Websites. They work in the CD-ROM drives on both PC and Macintosh platforms.

Computer-Telephony Integration. The convergence of two once-separate technologies—computing and telephony—and the most vital application service for next generation customer relationship solutions. CTI links your telephony resources, such as automated call distribution and your interactive voice response (IVR) system with your corporate information infrastructure.

Customer Management. Automates all the activities that an organization may have with its customers, including sales, telesales, marketing, telemarketing, customer service, and the help desk.

Campaign Management Software. An application that helps marketers plan, execute, evaluate, and refine marketing programs.

Database Management. Managing and synchronizing data stored in various databases to flow seamlessly and easily across the entire enterprise.

Data Mining. Extracting hidden predictive information from large databases and automatically detecting trends and associations hidden in data. Using a combination of machine learning, statistical analysis, modeling techniques, and database technology, data mining finds patterns and subtle relationships in data and infers rules that allow the prediction of future results. Typical applications include market segmentation, customer profiling, fraud detection, evaluation of retail promotions, and credit risk analysis.

Data Mart. A type of data warehouse designed primarily to address a specific function or department's needs, as opposed to a data warehouse, which is traditionally meant to address the needs of the organization from an enterprise perspective.

Data Warehouse. A system for storing and delivering massive quantities of data. Data warehouse software often includes sophisticated compression techniques for fast searches, as well as advanced filtering. A data warehouse is often remote so researchers can use it freely without slowing down day-to-day operations of the production database. Front-end decision support tools are used to access the data to produce useful information for selling, marketing, and servicing customers.

Enterprise Resource Planning (ERP). Positioned as the foundation and integration of enterprisewide information systems, this is sometimes described as the organization's IT "backbone." It provides users with the ability to interact with a common corporate database for a comprehensive range of applications managing financial, asset, and cost accounting; production operations and materials; personnel; plants; and archived documents.

Executive Information System. Analyzes performance, develops marketing plans, performs sales forecasting, and manages human resources.

Interactive voice response (IVR). A system that allows simple tasks to be executed either through touch-tone input or speech recognition, without the assistance of a live agent. This results in instant access to information for callers and greater call-handling capacity for companies, without additional staffing. Fax-on-demand is a natural next step. A customer can call an agent or an IVR system and retrieve sales literature, directions to a retail outlet, and price lists instantly and automatically by fax.

Internet. The world's largest TCP/IP network. Transmission control protocol/Internet protocol is a networking standard that forms the basis for the Internet, which has become a worldwide system of interconnected computer networks. The Internet is built on a series of protocols such as TCP/IP, HTTP, HTML, and FTP to provide an easy and powerful exchange of data and information.

Intranet. An internal system of connected networks built on Internet protocols and usually connected to the Internet via a firewall, that is, a computer insulating the internal network from the Internet. It allows only qualified traffic to pass in and out.

Knowledge Management. Represents a more humanistic approach to business process redesign than reengineering. Prescribed changes may be no less radical, but they use the organization's own assets to identify and correct process flaws. KM calls for equipping an organization with enterprise systems, interpersonal tools and mobile devices to integrate human insight with computer-processing power to measure results and provide continuous feedback. By applying knowledge, workers add their own contribution to it. KM's emphasis on revenue growth helps to foster worker buy-in.

Life-Cycle Management. The practice of tracking a customer through every stage of a relationship: initial contact, proposal, contract negotiation, commitment, delivery, installation, feedback, and, ideally, repeat sale.

Marketing Encyclopedia. A comprehensive database or collection of all current marketing and sales materials in an electronic format available via intranet, the Internet, or CD-ROM. Salespeople can use it to create customized presentations by selecting and organizing material. Content can include presentations, proposals, brochures, catalogs, service manuals, images, videos, and CAD drawings.

Sales Configurator. Allows salespeople to compare specifications and put together products, while providing pricing and identifying possible problems in production.

Sales Force Automation. Software and hardware that help qualify leads and keep contact information about existing accounts. It maintains the history of clients and lets managers track salespeople's activities. SFA may include contact managers, marketing encyclopedias, sales configuration, and order entry tools, but generally is designed for workflow applications.

Supply Chain Management Software. Identifies a company's business constraints through the supply chain, the series of process and suppliers that move products from raw materials to the arms of the customer. It helps salespeople make sure they can deliver a profitable product to a customer on time.

Synchronization. Applications that bring information from your legacy databases to agents' desktops as customer calls arrive or coordinate the updating of data on different databases.

Telemarketing/Telesales. Integrates with telephony or communications equipment such as ACD (automated call distributors) or IVR (integrated voice recognition) devices to support telephone sales efforts.

Workflow Management Software. Trains, organizes, and equips your sales team to function collaboratively—sharing information, knowledge, and information.

Chapter Ten

Selecting High Performers

"If a person is not performing, it is probably because they have been miscast for the job."

—W. Edwards Deming

- What traits should a company look for when hiring salespeople?
- How can an organization find the best sales candidates?
- What are some ways to encourage star salespeople to remain with your organization?

No sales strategy—no matter how carefully developed—can succeed without the support of a highly versatile and dedicated sales team. But as noted in earlier chapters, the traits that customers look for in a salesperson encompass much more than the ability to simply sell a product or service. Customers want to work with someone who understands their organizations' complex needs. They want a salesperson who can develop and deliver solutions that help their businesses grow; someone who approaches each opportunity as more of a partner than a supplier.

It's a pretty demanding position for any person to fill, but high-performing sales organizations realize that their immediate and long-term success rests on their ability to attract and hire exactly these kinds of salespeople. Some specialists even argue that the potential payoff to the organization of selecting successful salespeople may be greater than for any other occupation. A. J. Vinchur and his fellow researchers proposed this notion in a thought-provoking article in the *Journal of Applied Psychology*. After analyzing numerous studies, they reported, "The implication (from studies on job success) is that sales is an occupation in which any improvement in selection can have a major impact on the bottom line."[1]

The flip side of hiring the right person is the potential damage that the wrong selection can incur. In a Sales Success Profile study conducted by Lousig-Nont & Associates, a Las Vegas human resource consulting firm, managers revealed that their usual trial-and-error approach to hiring yielded an average turnover of 320 percent! Multiply this by the expense of training, and it becomes extremely costly to hire the wrong salespeople. Add to that the number of negative impressions that customers get from these undesirable individuals and you increase your losses even more.

Selecting and hiring the best possible salesperson is, of course, just the first step in building a winning sales team. To sustain high performance, organizations must also create strategies for retaining their sales talent. Few things are more frustrating for sales managers than expending major resources toward finding, hiring, and training salespeople who (sooner or later) leave for another position that offers greater personal satisfaction or a more acceptable compensation program. The loss of these salespeople not only puts the customer relationship at risk, but also incurs the considerable expense of replacing them. In fact, the cost of replacing a salesperson can be up to 10 times his or her annual salary.

There are almost as many selection and retention strategies as there are sales organizations. In this chapter, we've put together a composite of approaches used by a cross section of successful global organizations with varying recruiting needs.

ESTABLISHING THE HIRING CRITERIA

How should a company determine which attributes are most desirable in a salesperson?

For many sales managers, the answer is easy: the same attributes *they* have. Unfortunately, that answer fails to take into account the fact that today's salesperson most likely requires differ-

---

[1]A. J. Vinchur, J. S. Schippmann, F. S. Switzer III, and P. L. Roth, "A Meta-Analytic Review of Predictors of Job Performance for Salespeople," *Journal of Applied Psychology,* vol 83, no. 4, pp. 586–597.

ent competencies than those needed when the sales managers filled the position.

Even a profile of strictly positive personality traits can be misleading, since high and low achievers may identify many of the same characteristics. For example, a study of over 1000 of the best salespeople from 70 companies revealed that high achievers shared three key sales traits: strong objection-answering skills, good grooming habits, and conservative dress (especially, oddly enough, black shoes). A comparison study showed that the weakest performers at these same companies shared the same three traits.[2]

Another fallacy is that the typical interview process will winnow out the right person. Not necessarily, according to a University of Michigan study by John and Rhonda Hunter.[3] This research project examined how accurately job interviews predict job performance. *The findings:* The "typical" interview only increases the chances for choosing the best candidate by less than 2 percent. This surprisingly low rate of accuracy is primarily due to the fact that most managers take an informal and unplanned approach to interviewing with a vague, personal notion of the ideal candidate profile. Often, the applicant takes the lead and presents only his or her best attributes and experience. These kinds of interviews are most usually a waste of time for everyone involved—and could even be a harbinger of problems ahead if the interviewer is deceived and hires a candidate with the wrong skills or attributes.

Still another method for establishing the ideal sales candidate profile is to rely on the criteria established by others. For example, Vinchur et al. analyzed 100-plus studies that evaluated predictors for sales performance. The studies were conducted from as early as 1918 through 1996 and covered a wide range of sales positions, with insurance as the predominant industry. The authors concluded from this research that certain traits, such as extraversion and conscientiousness, could be strong indicators of sales success.

Some recruiting specialists, however, caution that success traits may differ too much from one organization to another to rely on universal results. Advantis, a research and consulting firm in Milwaukee, advocates the use of a "competency model" based on traits *and* behaviors critical to success for that specific organization and its

---

[2]Howard Stevens, "Smart Hiring: How to Avoid the Most Common Sales Hiring Errors," *Selling Power* (September 1998).

[3]Ibid.

specific customers. Traits are characteristics—such as optimism or initiative—that are hard, if not impossible, to acquire through training. Behaviors are measurable factors critical to success—such as precall planning, time management, and follow-up—that *can* be acquired through training. To develop a competency model, sales executives, salespeople, and even customers can be surveyed to develop a profile of a high performer.

Asha Knutsen, a vice president at Advantis, says that companies can use these competency models to develop tools to aid in the recruiting and interviewing process and beyond. Recently, Advantis used this approach to help select candidates for the particularly tough job of "team salesperson." The model allows for identification of a variety of competencies required for the team to function effectively. Each person on the team does not need to possess all the competencies, only those important to his or her role. But when the entire team is assembled, the model ensures that *all* the traits and behaviors required are present. The effectiveness of this approach can then be validated through sales results, customer feedback, and 360-degree feedback studies. Knutsen says that there is a trend toward "integrated" competency models as "Velcro" for attracting, hiring, and retaining salespeople. Integrating the selection, hiring, performance management, training and development, career planning, and succession planning of salespeople can all be based on a competency model of the successful salesperson for that organization.

To establish reliable criteria for hiring the right salesperson, many organizations rely on validation studies rather than surveys.

Validation studies compare statistically comprehensive enough samples of high and low performers to discover which factors unfailingly distinguish high performers from average performers in a specific sales environment. These factors are then checked against specific performance criteria, such as actual sales results, to identify the precise skills and traits that will predict success in that environment.[4]

---

[4]Stevens, *Selling Power.*

Caution

When establishing your ideal candidate profile, don't get carried away with the number of skills and traits (factors) you prescribe for success. Researchers claim that the most accurate prediction of on-the-job performance should include no more than six to eight factors. Otherwise, you end up with a watered-down version of a top performer. Success factors will vary from company to company, based on such considerations as corporate culture, product lines, sales force responsibilities and autonomy, and customer base.

Another interesting and important thing to keep in mind when establishing your criteria is that the number-one trait that predicts success for your salespeople is usually as important or more important than all others combined.[5]

With a validated set of criteria in hand, a clear profile of the successful salesperson emerges. A sales manager can then measure all candidates against this profile and accurately assess their potential. In addition, this profile gives the employer a real appraisal of the candidate's competency against top performers already employed by the company. For example, a useful observation that may be drawn in this way might be something like, "This applicant has demonstrated skills in previous positions that are equal to or better than the skills demonstrated by 50 percent of our present sales force." A validated profile can also help design an interview tool as described above.

Two Critical Attributes

The methods for selecting top salespeople run the gamut from competency modeling and standard interview techniques to psychological testing, handwriting analysis, and lie detector tests. Whatever method is used, however, our research shows that there are two key attributes that high-performance sales companies typically look for when hiring new salespeople: experience and values.

Experience. In today's competitive environment, companies have little time for salespeople to ramp up on product and industry knowledge. They need salespeople who thoroughly understand the customers' requirements—practically from day one. When a customer

---

[5]Ibid.

and salesperson meet for the first time, the customer is already measuring that salesperson's understanding of the industry and ability to add value by responding to specific business needs and objectives. They want a valued business consultant, not just a salesperson.

Our research of top sales organizations worldwide found that three factors that most influence the salesperson's ability to fulfill the role of a valued business consultant:

- *Knowledge:* Customers want salespeople to help them make effective business decisions based on an understanding of the business environment.

- *Communication skills* enable the salesperson to convey clearly and accurately all the information needed to make these decisions.

- *A positive attitude* includes such personal traits as sensitivity, enthusiasm, and integrity.

Customers today have many more choices for fulfilling their product and service needs. Most companies can match product quality and operational excellence. However, a knowledgeable and dedicated sales force will give these companies the competitive edge. Customers need a salesperson that can advise them on the best way to use products and services to increase success with their own customers. If your organization can offer such support and experience, it will clearly distinguish itself from other companies in the marketplace.

Therefore, when searching for salespeople, look for individuals who have direct experience within your customers' industries. With that foundation, they can more quickly add value to your customers and understand the application of your products and services to their business needs. Jeff Worth, Vice President of Sales and Marketing for Castrol Industrial North America's Performance Lubricants division says that this is a critical factor in Castrol's hiring decisions.

"Understanding the needs of the customer is primary for any successful sales approach," he says. "We prefer to spend our training time and dollars focusing on a consistent approach for "how" to sell, not ramping the salesperson up on industry knowledge."

This experience can benefit the sales organization as well, by bringing competitive intelligence, industry trends insight, and customer application information. "We benefit from the industry knowledge a salesperson brings," Worth adds. "We tend to hire people with a minimum of five years' experience in the industry."

Values. Ethics and integrity are becoming important issues with customers who must rely on salespeople for counsel and support. In high-performance sales organizations, a new breed of sales advisors armed with consultative skills, knowledge, and honesty is fast replacing the negative stereotypes that earlier plagued even the best of salespeople.

The Sales Success Profile study mentioned earlier, surveyed over 1200 businesses to determine common qualities shared by successful salespersons. In addition to the traditional categories of prospecting and cold calls, qualifying, overcoming objections, and closing, sales managers in the study also listed specific "people skills" needed by successful salespeople. These included courtesy, warmth and friendliness, problem handling, call enthusiasm, and—notably—high ethics. One conclusion that may be drawn from these findings: If you hire people who truly believe in your products, they will more likely remain with your company and promote it in an honest, above-board manner. If salespeople don't believe they are backing something of high value, how can they present that product with conviction? As a customer of Allen and Hanbury's stated, "[top Salesperson] is honest about the product. He admits what it can't do as well as what it can do."

Our own research indicates that the attitudes of top salespeople focus in no small part on selling with a sense of values. The best ones, said one surveyed manager, are so concerned about helping the customer, they actually forget they're selling. Added a sales manager from Northwestern Mutual, "[top salespeople] don't think of what they are selling. They don't think: 'I'm going to sell you a policy.' "

DEVELOPING AN EFFECTIVE RECRUITING STRATEGY

Once the ideal candidate profile has been drawn up, high performance sales organizations follow a consistent, highly structured approach to recruiting the desired candidates. For internal candidates 3M Singapore offers new or challenging assignments in addition to their existing responsibilities. This helps them develop their potential and equips them with the skill and knowledge they'll need if they take on the new assignment.

Regarding the hiring of outside candidates, there are as many methods as there are companies. A typical strategy follows a four-step process:

1. Put out a wide net to find qualified candidates.
2. Narrow your pool of candidates through effective interviewing.
3. Look for a mix of performers.
4. Check them out before making the offer.

Put Out a Wide Net to Find Qualified Candidates

How do you go about finding these salespeople who have the knowledge, skills, and values that you want representing your company? Most high performance sales organizations we've worked with spread out a large "sourcing net." One of the most common ways they do this is by implementing an employee referral program. Companies find time and again that high performers know and associate with other high performers. Some organizations find it beneficial to compensate employees who refer individuals who successfully complete a prespecified period of employment.

They also check with noncompeting vendors about possible candidates. If these vendors serve the same marketplace, they can recommend salespeople who already know the appropriate products or services and customers. As in many other situations, networking can be very helpful in providing valuable contacts and information.

Another valuable and increasingly utilized source for highly qualified, successful candidates nationwide is the Internet. The Internet has made sourcing of candidates a great deal easier, particularly if a company is willing to pay for relocation. Many organizations' Websites have separate sections for job seekers, providing information about the company and its employment opportunities. Some even list specific jobs or a general overview of the types of positions available, including details on the skills needed and the characteristics their validation research found as desirable. To get qualified candidates to locate their sites, these Web-savvy organizations create links with search engines and employment sites. Many high-tech firms, for example, have experienced good results using the Monster Board and other Websites featuring job openings and résumé postings.

Executive search firms are a tried-and-true way to uncover talent. Many companies will pay a portion of the salesperson's first-year earnings to outsource the search process. This allows companies to contact experienced, qualified candidates within customer organizations or competitors, without making the initial contact directly.

Putting out a wide net does not always mean simply trying to uncover as many candidates as possible. Some organizations begin the winnowing process even as they cast the net out. Where and how a company recruits can narrow the type of candidate they attract. Often, companies utilize their human resource function to filter through résumés, eliminating the ones that don't meet some preidentified criteria or possess identified traits. Many sales managers will then interview only qualified candidates, thereby saving time and effort, yet still reserving the "judgement calls" for themselves rather than human resources.

Narrow Your Pool of Candidates through Effective Interviewing

Once a company has compiled a list of potential candidates from various sourcing and recruiting vehicles, interviewing begins. And here's exactly where so many recruiting efforts go wrong. As noted earlier, without developing a structured and consistent interview, no organization can bank on hiring candidates who match its hiring needs. A strong set of criteria based on a competency model is critical in the interview process and should be used to develop a tool to guide each interviewer through the interviewing process. A competency-based interview tool would include predeveloped probes that help the interviewer zero in on two key areas:

1. Specific past experiences and examples of performance in a given competency area
2. Potential for future performance around an area of importance

This approach ensures that the interview stays on track and that the person conducting the interview is able to gather information necessary to compare candidates to each other, rather than simply focusing on personality or allowing the candidate to drive the interview. Information about each candidate is then compiled and compared objectively to other candidates, focusing on the critical competencies.

In *Sales and Marketing Management Magazine*, Michelle Marchetti offers the example of Edward Jones, a financial services company in St. Louis. Edward Jones hired the Gallup Organization to create a composite profile, which identified the sales pros as persistent, self-reliant, and "willing to bet it all on themselves."

Each month, Edward Jones combs through approximately 1000 applications, 80 percent of which are referrals from their own sales force. The company looks specifically for candidates who are excelling in their current position but are frustrated with the compensation, as well as those who have risen both in rank and pay level. Gallup calls the individuals who make the cut, asking them 60 questions aimed at uncovering three key personality traits: strong work ethic, high degree of motivation, and the ability to build rapport.

Salespeople who demonstrate these qualities are given personal interviews, which may uncover competencies identified in the profile. About 200, or 20 percent of the total applicant pool, are hired. Over the four-plus years since Edward Jones implemented this new hiring approach, the company's attrition rate has fallen from 20.8 to 9 percent![6]

Look for a Mix of Performers

According to Howard Stevens, CEO of the H. R. Chally Group, it's important a company looks for more than "number 10s" in the interviewing process. Often, he says, sales organizations want to hire all superstars—"A" performers or career salespeople who come by selling naturally and will succeed no matter what support the employer does or does not provide. This is an unrealistic expectation. "If you have one in a hundred salespeople that fit into this superstar category, you are very lucky," said Stevens.

Ideally, according to Stevens, a sales force should consist mostly of B and C salespeople. B performers are bright, capable, and motivated, but destined to move on to other avenues. Companies should make sure that these grade B performers compose only 5 to 9 percent of their sales force, or training and development dollars could go sky high. The C performers are capable salespeople, often motivated by external forces. With the right support, they will provide above-average sales results. These individuals, Stevens says, should compose 80 to 90 percent of an organization's sales force.

---

[6]Michelle Marchetti, Chad Kayto. "Give us 2 weeks and we'll give you a new sales force." *Sales and Marketing Management* (Dec. 1998), p. 31.

D performers may have some skills, but they also have a fatal flaw: They are weak on follow-up or lack discipline. F performers present a real danger. They may have legal issues or be con artists. *Hirer, beware:* These D and F candidates often perform very well in interviews and even on background checks. Through validated testing, which focuses on motivation and competency, a company should be able to identify—and avoid—these potential threats.

Check Them Out before Making an Offer

No hiring method—including the development of an ideal candidate profile, interviewing or testing—is foolproof. Reference checks are an additional test most every organization claims it uses as part of the hiring test. But according to an article in *Selling Power,*[7] placement agencies report a high percentage of false information in résumés. As many as 15 to 20 percent of job applicants try to hide something negative in their past. For some positions, one out of three resumes may contain false information!

The moral of the story: Never take a candidate's word as validation of qualifications and experience. Do a reference check—and check sources in addition to those provided by the candidate. The approach taken for confirming references varies from company to company. Michael Zinn, president of an executive search consulting firm in New York and New Jersey, says that a good reference-checking process includes three elements:

- *General background check* This includes a credit check, a DMV check, and a background check for felonies and misdemeanors.

- *Selected References* Zinn suggests sending candidates a structured sheet asking for names and contact information of the last five people they reported to, plus the nature of the organizational relationship and dates of employment. He advises against letting candidates choose their references. Similarly, send a form asking for contact information and names of subordinates and peers. Calling these 10 or so individuals will allow you to observe behavioral patterns. Too often, companies rely on just two or three decent references instead of three times that amount. The latter will present a much clearer picture of the individual.

---

[7] Jon P. Steinbrink, "How to Pay Your Sales Force," *Harvard Business Review,* 1989.

- *Informal References*   Zinn suggests that, with the candidate's permission, it's a good idea to call the candidate's trusted friends and customers for more informal references. Several types of questions are appropriate here. These include: how long have they known the person and through what circumstances, the person's strengths and weaknesses, projects with which the candidate was involved and individual contributions, how the person confronted and approached challenges and problems, and how they would describe the candidate's written reports and presentation style.

Jeff Worth, Vice President of Sales and Marketing of Castrol Industrial North America, believes strongly in checking on candidates. Castrol hires an outside firm to do this. Sometimes, Worth believes, candidates are not what they appear to be in an interview. "People will sometimes present an image of themselves that isn't always real," he says. "We want to make sure that the image the candidate is presenting is what they really are."

ATTRACTING HIGH PERFORMERS

To attract high performers, companies should take a marketing, rather than recruiting, approach. The companies best at attracting high performers, particularly in a tight labor market, according to Kevin Klinvex of Select International, a selection and recruiting firm, use a practice he calls "extreme recruiting."

"With extreme recruiting, recruiters act more like marketers and less like recruiters," he says. Organizations can no longer be satisfied with putting a want ad in the paper. Klinvex urges more creative approaches involving public relations, marketing, and "good ambassadorship."

"The first rule to attracting talented performers is to portray the organization as a desirable place to work," he says. "The more creative ways an organization can find to do that, the more effective their recruiting efforts—and performance as a whole—will be."

Kim Kleps, Vice President of Training and Performance Development at Frontier Communications, says that the fact that Frontier offers salespeople quality training in both selling skills and technical knowledge to differentiate themselves demonstrates that the company values its salespeople as an important asset for the organization. "When our recruiters are out in the community, it is a contributing factor that makes their jobs easier."

Other tips from Kevin Klinvex of Select International include

- Establish a task force to brainstorm ways to attract top talent.
- Use the Internet both to make your presence known and to find potential hires.
- Use alternative media to get your message out—everything from radio spots to billboards.
- Advertise in different sections of the newspaper, not just the classifieds.
- Make the interview process quick and efficient, as salespeople get fed up with too many interviews (three should be enough).

Klinvex says that the most important factor in attracting top performers is making *everyone* in the organization responsible for recruiting—not just human resources or a few sales executives. "Incentives for employee referrals really work," he says, "but the reward should be meaningful. For a talented employee who stays, a referral reward of $5,000 to $10,000 is not uncommon. If you want employees to recruit for the company, make the incentive worth their while."

RETAINING HIGH PERFORMERS

Top sales organizations know that hiring the desired candidate is just the first step in an effective hiring and retention process. 3M Singapore cites clear career paths, plenty of career opportunities, fast-track promotions, and recognition programs as key aspects of their strategy for retaining high performers. They also include in their yearly assessments of their salespeople a review of each salesperson's strengths, development needs, and achievements. In this way, they help improve morale and reduce turnover.

The high cost of turnover alone makes it imperative to keep high performers happy, wanting to stay with the organization for their entire sales careers. While that may be an unrealistic goal in today's evolving work environment, most high performance sales organizations strive for that objective by focusing on three key components of an effective retention strategy:

- Motivation
- Compensation
- Support and recognition

Motivation

In their study, "What Counts Most in Motivating Your Sales Force," funded by the Associates of the Harvard Business School and Western Electric Fund, Stephen X. Doyle and Benson P. Shapiro found that there is no one simple solution to motivating salespeople. The more successful sales executives recognize that motivation is largely a result of a combination of effective recruiting practices, sensible pay plans and good management."[8]

Doyle and Shapiro's study looked at how much personality, incentive pay, task clarity, and good management impact the level of motivation. They conducted in-depth interviews with salespeople and their managers, analyzed a questionnaire filled out by over 200 salespeople in four organizations, and observed numerous sales calls. The results showed that two of the most important determinants of motivation are:

1. *The nature of the task, or the description of the sales job itself.* The study indicated that clarity of the sales task is strongly related to on-the-job performance and effort. If the sales task is unclear, the salesperson will not be able to pinpoint the results of personal efforts. This "disconnect" is frustrating and lessens the self-esteem that could come from accomplishment. Clear tasks ensure that the linkage between the effort expended and the actual sales results is tight.

2. *Personality, particularly the strength of the salesperson's need for achievement.* Doyle and Shapiro found a direct correlation between the degree of a person's need for achievement and level of motivation. As need for achievement increases, so do effort and motivation. The need for achievement makes good salespeople, who thrive in a system where the effort they expend clearly relates to results.

Compensation

Over the years, many studies have also looked at the type of compensation programs that are most effective. In another Harvard study, John P. Steinbrink looked at three basic compensation plans: salary, commission, and combination (salary plus incentive) plans.

---

[8]*Harvard Business Review* (May/June, 1980), p. 133.

All of these approaches, he stated, have both advantages and disadvantages for the sales force and company. The best approach depends on several factors: "A properly designed and implemented compensation plan must be geared both to the needs of the company and to the products or services the company sells," Steinbrink writes. "At the same time, it must attract good salespeople in the first place and then keep them producing at increasing rates." In order to retain high performers, Castrol Industrial North America matches compensation to performance. Salespeople are paid on 100 percent commission, and that commission is related to profit margin. In this way, says Jeff Worth, "salespeople feel they are a direct part of the company's and their own success."

Doyle and Shapiro's study determined that, in general, incentive pay is more effective than straight salary and, more importantly, that the impact of the incentive pay is greater when the sales task is clear. Incentive compensation strongly links reward and recognition. Their study also emphasized that, when it comes to compensation, it is critical to have accurate reporting of actual sales results, as well as equitable rewards and valuable recognition of those results. They concluded that the most successful managers adopt a multifunctional incentive approach to achieve the greatest possible improvement in sales performance:

Salesperson effort expended

↓

Actual sales results

Reported sales results

Rewards and recognition

Steinbrink reinforces the point made by Doyle and Shapiro that no matter how well a compensation plan is formulated and executed, other incentives are needed as well. These include a combination of financial motivators such as short-term contests and nonfinancial ones such as honorary titles, sales awards, and personal letters or telephone calls of recognition and commendation.

Cypress Semiconductor

In the competitive world of high technology, customers aren't the only ones worth fighting for. High performing salespeople are as important to a company as any other of its assets. In a tight labor market, and a demanding field, Cypress Semiconductor found itself looking for ways to attract and retain committed, motivated, and skilled salespeople.

"We looked at the whole package we offer to salespeople—from the way we attract and recruit, to the way we hire, all the way through to the way we train and compensate. We knew that if we wanted to attract the best people, and have them stay, we had to make an investment in all of these areas" says Bill Bradford, Director of Sales for the Eastern United States. And invest they have. Cypress set about a process of studying and benchmarking themselves against competitors, interviewing salespeople, conducting focus groups, and forming task forces to determine how to recruit, hire, train, and retain the best people.

To attract and hire high performers, Cypress developed a competency-based profile, which outlines the requirements for the role that the salesperson will play in the organization. Cypress then trained a significant number of managers in the most effective way to interview to these competencies. "This helps to avoid people relying on their favorite interview questions, which may have nothing to do with what we are looking for." They also branched out, and began recruiting from universities and then offering extensive training for those hired.

Cypress and the newly hired salesperson then commit to "The Deal," a progressive agreement between company and employee that demonstrates what support the organization will provide and what the salesperson will do to ensure mutual success and satisfaction. "The Deal" focuses on four quadrants: Compensation, Recognition, Training and Development, and Interesting/Challenging Work. Cypress determined through its research that their compensation was competitive and their work was challenging and interesting. They then set out to work on the other two.

(continued)

Cypress Semiconductor (concluded)

In the past year, Cypress has instituted a curriculum of training for salespeople and sales managers that delivers the critical skills for salespeople to work with their customers and for sales managers to coach for results. The training, and even performance reviews, link back to the competencies originally outlined for the hiring process—a truly integrated system. Combined with some new recognition and mentoring programs, these efforts are already seeing positive results.

Support and Recognition

Our own studies and experience with high-performance sales organizations have found several other noncompensation-related factors that increase a salesperson's job satisfaction and his or her desire to remain with the company. The first is a clear sales process. This correlates to the findings of Doyle and Shapiro regarding the clarity of the task. As we noted in earlier chapters, in a top sales organization, all employees are familiar with the organization's sales strategy and can develop activities that support this strategy. Everyone also understands the specific approaches or processes that are in place to meet the customer's needs.

A particularly effective technique for understanding the customer's needs and supporting the sales effort is *Sales Performance Process Mapping.* This technique consists of an entire sequence of person-to-person business encounters that a customer experiences when interacting with a sales organization. Every organization has its own particular process. If it is well understood companywide, it can be critiqued and improved on a regular basis (See Chapter 4).

Training is another important factor that impacts turnover, says Curtis E. Plott, president of the American Society for Training and Development in Alexandria, Virginia. Training, he notes, may actually be one of the best investments a company can make, since it can help create a bond between the company and employees and encourage valued personnel to remain (See Chapter 11). For example, several years ago, Taco Inc., a manufacturer of heating and cooling equipment in Cranston, Rhode Island, established a Taco Learning

Center on its premises with two classrooms, a computer lab room, a library, and a conference room. The result: employee turnover declined to an all-time low. (Nation's Business).[9] Kim Kleps of Frontier agrees that training impacts retention. "Salespeople at Frontier are given the skills and tools they need to differentiate themselves from competitors. Because of this, they are more successful. This of course impacts their desire to stay with our company."

CONCLUSION

The days of the one-dimensional "sell, sell, sell" salesperson are history. Today, success comes to those organizations that focus on building relationships with their customers. This requires people with strong leadership skills, business acumen, interpersonal and facilitation skills, and teamwork ability. Progressive organizations now realize that they must attract, hire, and retain individuals who understand and look forward to accepting their new responsibilities and challenges.

It's always been important to hire and retain top performers. Today, with the added dimension of ever-escalating customer expectations, hiring the *right* person has become even more essential. To build strong, long-lasting relationships with successful salespeople, a company must put into place a clear sales-recruiting process that is communicated companywide. It should clearly define the traits expected from the sales force and the ways that each person will be rewarded or compensated for positive results.

Salespeople should be able to clearly describe their job tasks, territory, customer base, and performance goals so they can see the relationship between their efforts and results.

It's also important that companies define, through validity studies models and measurement, the skills expected from their sales force. This will help them source and recruit individuals who match their organization's needs and possess those traits that correlate to

---

[9]Michael Barrier. "Closing the Skills Gap." *Nation's Business* (March 1996), p. 26.

success. This will also help ensure that all salespeople recognize what constitutes top performance and will continue to work toward that goal.

BEST PRACTICES AND GUIDING PRINCIPLES

- Develop a competency model, based on traits and behaviors critical to success in a specific sales discipline, to be used during the hiring process.
- Use validation studies to establish an ideal candidate profile.
- When establishing an ideal candidate profile, limit your "requirements" to no more than six to eight factors; otherwise, you end up with a watered-down version of a top performer.
- Remember that when establishing your criteria, the number-one trait that predicts success for your salespeople is usually as important or more important than all other factors combined.
- Experience and values are the two key attributes that high performance sales companies look for when hiring new salespeople.
- Look for salespeople with experience within your customers' industries.
- Regarding values, remember that the salespeople are so concerned about helping customers that they sometimes actually forget they're selling.
- To develop an effective recruiting strategy:

  Put out a wide net to find qualified candidates.

  Narrow your pool of candidates through effective interviewing.

  Look for a mix of performers.

  Check them out before making the offer.

- Use the Web: It is fast becoming an excellent source of qualified candidates.
- When interviewing, develop probes that uncover:

  Specific past experiences and examples of performance in a given competency area.

  Potential for future performance around an area of importance.

- Look for a mix of performers. Remember that a sales force of all A performers is probably both unrealistic and counterproductive, since A performers tend to be mavericks. Organizations need steady contributors as well as home-run hitters.
- Never take a candidate's word as validation of qualifications and experience. Conduct thorough background checks.
- To attract high performers, try extreme recruiting, in which recruiters act more like marketers and less like recruiters.
- To retain high performers, make sure you motivate, compensate, support, and recognize your sales force appropriately.

Chapter Eleven

Strategic Sales Training

"Properly training salespeople to make sure they can effectively compete is one of the biggest challenges facing companies today."

—Sales manager, Xerox Corporation
(United States)

- What is strategic sales training?
- How can training help to communicate a strategic vision?
- Is there a model for strategic training?
- What are the characteristics of strategic training?
- What are some trends in training?

The concepts and ideas that we've discussed so far in this book—customer loyalty; consultative selling; technology; hiring; and the salesperson as strategic orchestrator, business consultant, and long-term ally—are powerful strategies used by the world's top-performing sales organizations to achieve competitive differentiation. These strategies are brought to life and executed consistently by salespeople who understand the implications for their daily sales practices. One of the most powerful methods to achieve this is strategic sales training.

ONE VISION, CLEARLY COMMUNICATED

"Our sales training is directed at the critical strategic areas of our business."

—Vice president, Bayerische Vereinsbank
(Germany)

Sales Training

The process of providing a salesperson or sales team member with the skills, knowledge, and attitudes necessary to increase that person's productivity.

Strategic Sales Training

The use of sales training to achieve a sales strategy in a systematic way.

Sales executives and training managers at top-performing organizations agree that the best sales training decisions are linked to an organization's key business objectives.

To establish this link at your company, each person in your sales and sales training organizations should be able to answer the following question:

How should our salespeople sell differently to meet the changing market conditions of today and tomorrow?

Some organizations have been able to answer this in a way that is easily understood at all levels. In doing so, these companies create a common language in which all employees discuss the organization's sales strategy and develop activities that support that strategy. Creating this kind of unity requires tremendous focus, discipline, and leadership.

Hewlett-Packard (United States) is one company that has achieved this common understanding and commitment. Every person we interviewed at Hewlett-Packard expressed a clear understanding of the company's competitive issues and goals and their sales organization's key strategies. Most strikingly, three levels of sales managers, several sales representatives, and the vice president of sales all described the sales strategy using similar words and phrases. Moreover, each had a clear understanding of the tasks they needed to complete to help achieve the company's objectives.

Another example of this kind of organizationwide understanding is Northwestern Mutual Life Insurance Company (United States), where the company mission statement—written by its founders in 1888—is still relevant today:

> The ambition of The Northwestern has been less to be large than to
> be safe; its aim is to rank first in benefits to policy owners rather than
> first in size. Valuing quality above quantity, it has preferred to secure
> its business under certain salutary restrictions and limitations rather
> than to write a much larger business at the possible sacrifice of those
> valuable points which have made The Northwestern preeminently
> the policy owner's company.

Northwestern Mutual's mission statement guides the daily activities of all its divisions and departments, serving as a philosoph-
ical and ethical cornerstone and a clear statement about their values.

A key strength at these and other top sales organizations is that
sales-training directors are as familiar with their company's business strategies as sales executives and the line operation. The
sales-training directors have an understanding of how their company's markets are changing, the sales strategies being used to
adapt to those changes, and the roles that salespeople have to fulfill to execute the sales strategies. They are able to discuss the competencies as well as the design and implementation issues of a
training solution.

As Table 11-1 reveals, sales executives, sales-operations managers, and sales-training managers must share a vision of the markets, strategies, and appropriate training responses if the company
is to successfully meet its objectives.

Where there is no shared vision, confusion and mixed signals
reign. Sales executives may mistakenly believe that they are providing enough information to guide decisions about training. Some
sales-training managers may sense that they are missing information but aren't sure how to describe what they're missing.

In fact, every organization intends its sales training to support its
sales strategies. The greatest risk for any organization is to assume
that this is happening. One training manager we met talked at
length about his company's training programs, schedules, and the
number of hours of training each salesperson receives. But he was
much less specific, and clearly uncomfortable, when asked how
sales training was able to help his company differentiate itself from
competition or to bring a specific strategy to life.

TABLE 11-1
Ideal Profile of Shared Information

Area	Sales Executives	Sales Operations	Sales Training Groups
How markets are changing	√	√	√
How sales strategies are changing	√	√	√
The new roles of the salesperson	√	√	√
How salespeople must sell differently	√	√	√
New skills, knowledge, and attitudes	—	√	√
Designing, implementing, assessing, and improving training	—	—	√

DYNAMIC MARKETS, CHANGING NEEDS: MODEL FOR STRATEGIC SALES TRAINING

"We use sales training to respond to the increasing challenge of our markets."

—Vice president, Scott Paper Company
(United States)

Today's volatile markets and intense competition often require dramatic and rapid changes in an organization's sales strategy, changing the essential nature of the sales calls that the organization's salespeople conduct with customers.

Many organizations today are focusing on time-based strategies such as reducing cycle times to increase their responsiveness to market opportunities. As Stalk and Hout proposed in *Competing Against Time*, the results of compressing time are impressive. As time is compressed, the following changes occur:

- Productivity increases.
- Prices can be increased.
- Risks are reduced.
- Share is increased.[1]

---

[1]George Stalk, Jr., and Thomas M. Hout, *Competing Against Time* (New York: The Free Press), 1990.

Strategic sales training plays a role in supporting time-based competition by ensuring that strategies are communicated and executed quickly and consistently.

To make sure that sales training is relevant and focuses on today's strategies and practices, sales-training directors in the leading sales organizations are taking the initiative to ensure that they have a current comprehensive understanding of today's sales strategies. Based on our discussions with them, and on our own experience developing and implementing sales training, we have developed a model for strategic sales training (see Table 11-2). Executing each of these steps well will help ensure that your sales training directly supports your sales strategy. Each of these activities is crucial to achieving effective strategic sales training. If any of these steps is skipped or executed poorly, the effectiveness will be diminished.

The strategic sales-training model illustrates how to use training as a critical tool that brings a sales strategy to life. Training can be used to communicate a strategy and define what the salespeople need to do to sell successfully.

SYSTEMATIC TRAINING PLAN

"The purpose of training is to provide practice. Otherwise, we have to practice on customers."

—Vice president, American Airlines
(United States)

For generations, many sales organizations have been staunch advocates of on-the-job training for salespeople. They emphasized the fact that the most effective way for salespeople to improve was through experience, and that their skills would be sharpened over time as they gained more experience in working with actual customers.

But in today's market, customers simply cannot afford to be tutors for salespeople. They have too many pressures of their own, and they can't afford the time needed to "break in" a new salesperson for a supplier organization. Nor can they tolerate the ripple effect that a new salesperson's mistakes could have.

Most sales organizations can't afford this risk, either. The sink-or-swim approach of on-the-job training puts unnecessary strain on a customer relationship—if it doesn't break it entirely. Leading sales

TABLE 11-2
A Model for Strategic Sales Training

Activities	*Key Questions*
1. Describe company strategy.	What changes are occurring in the market regarding customers, technology, and competition?
	What is our strategy to differentiate us from competition?
2. Describe sales strategy.	How will the sales organization help differentiate the company?
	How can the sales organization add value beyond that already provided by products and services?
3. Build commitment to the strategies.	Does everyone in the sales organization have a common understanding of the company strategy and the sales strategy?
	Does everyone have a high level of commitment?
	Is there an understanding of how the organization, and every individual, will benefit from supporting the strategy?
4. Identify new roles.	What new roles will your salespeople fulfill to execute the sales strategy?
	Are the roles of strategic orchestrator, business consultant, and long-term ally important?
5. Determine new ways of selling.	How will salespeople have to sell differently to carry out the new roles?
	What competencies (knowledge, skills, and attitudes) do salespeople need to sell differently?
	Will activities in the Customer Relationship Process require new competencies?
6. Identify training needs.	What are competency strengths and weaknesses?
	What competencies should the training target for improvement?

(continued)

TABLE 11-2—*(continued)*
A Model for Strategic Sales Training

Activities	Key Questions
7. Describe ideal training design.	What content and methodology should be included?
8. Implement training.	How can the quality of implementation be ensured?
	How can learning be reinforced?
	What coaching and follow-up activities are intended?
9. Assess training.	Is new learning being used on the job? What is the impact?
10. Improve training.	What needs to be improved, and how can it be done?

organizations have found that a better alternative to practicing in front of customers is to have their salespeople practice in structured settings with other salespeople: in a word, training.

"Training gives salespeople confidence, product knowledge, and a structure to implement it in front of a customer," noted a field sales manager from Allen & Hanbury's (United Kingdom). "People have to get better to survive in more difficult market situations," added a vice president from Océ (France). "One of the ways that they can improve is through training."

The sales organizations that are the most satisfied with their training share the following characteristics:

1. *Sales training is linked to a sales strategy.* Communications about the training make a clear link between the strategy and the training. Any case studies and examples used in the training are relevant to the strategy, as are the skills, knowledge, and attitudes taught in the training.

2. Training is designed, planned, and implemented to achieve specific objectives. The expectations and goals for the training are clearly stated.

3. *Training is implemented as a continuous process.* Training is provided at regular intervals throughout each salesperson's career.

*Frontier Communications Forges Ahead of Competition with New
Sales Skills*

The technology explosion of data and the Internet has caused dramatic changes in the telecommunications industry. New technologies, products, and services are being developed at a frantic pace. For
Frontier Communications to stay ahead of the pack, it had to become
more data-centric and customer-focused. Significant strides in technical and product training were needed to equip salespeople with
timely competitive information. Salespeople needed new skills for
working with customers whose businesses were also undergoing
significant changes in how they operate and how they intend to communicate in the future.

"We have been searching for more innovative ways to be a more
market-driven, more profitable telecommunications company. Differentiation in the plethora of competitors out there is critical," says Donna
Reeves, president of sales for Frontier Communications. "An integrated, systematic training approach is helping us to accomplish that."

Frontier defined and documented its sales performance process to
align it with the multimillion dollar investment it was making
in sales force automation tools. Frontier personnel also designed,
planned, and implemented training around the entire sales-
performance process.

Product training was streamlined, the company's intranet was
put to use, and the training was integrated with new selling skills
language. When new products were launched, salespeople practiced
probing strategies and dealing with customer objections.

The changes went far beyond courses and learning. Frontier required a cultural shift. They needed to engage many functional
groups within the organization to get the maximum payback on
their sales-training investment. The sales-training team became involved with various corporate initiatives that only months prior
would have been off limits. The training team influenced performance appraisals, rewards, recognition, compensation, hiring and pro-
motion practices, organizational structure, processes, and policies
and aligned these systems with sales-training initiatives.

Frontier developed reinforcement and coaching mechanisms. It
gained sales training reinforcement commitment from sales management as well as the entire executive leadership team.

(continued)

Frontier Communications Forges Ahead of Competition with New Sales Skills (concluded)

"We knew that in order to effectively drive a behavioral transformation we had to link our training to the defined sales strategy and achieve very specific and stated objectives. It would be critical that our training become a continuous process, not just a few flashes in the pan," says Kim Kleps, Vice President of Training and Performance Development.

Managers were identified as pivotal to the link between training and corporate strategy. In a speech to managers, Donna Reeves said, "As a sales leader, you play a critical role in both rep productivity and employee retention. And one thing is crystal clear; our employees are thirsty for motivation, direction, and leadership. And they are looking at you and me to deliver that. It is our responsibility. We need to start doing things differently. Your responsibility as a manager goes beyond hitting the numbers. So, we as a corporation are changing the way we define your role as a sales leader. Every day, you should be modeling, coaching, motivating, recognizing, and evaluating. You need to be spending more face-to-face time with your people, keeping them informed. It's your job to communicate and support Frontier's strategy and vision—to lead by example."

The senior team consistently "kicked off" manager meetings and the meeting agenda connected with training and the corporate objectives.

As Frontier begins to define the "new frontier," their sales organization is poised to capitalize on the communications revolution with increased sales productivity, from $440 million in 1987 to $667 million in 1998.

4. *Training is supported with follow-up and coaching.*
   Reinforcement and applications workshops help ensure that new skills learned during the training are actually practiced on the job. Salespeople receive feedback on their performance during regular sales coaching calls.

5. *Sales policies and procedures are consistent with the objectives of the training.* Sales compensation, for example, does not encourage or tempt salespeople to work with their accounts in ways that are different from the practices they learned in training.

TRENDS IN TRAINING

"The ultimate training is just-in-time and just-for-me."

—Director of PHH University, PHH Corporation
(United States)

Sales training plays an important role within each of the sales organizations that participated in the sales leadership research. That role is changing every day as business pressures and available opportunities change. The following are some important trends in training.

Different segments and channels will require different training

"The important thing about training is what can I do with it tomorrow and the day after?"

—Training manager, Océ
(The Netherlands)

The increased costs of face-to-face selling will cause organizations to segment and target their customers more specifically in both business and consumer sales. Telemarketing and alternative distribution channels will be used more often. Training will support the skills and abilities required for success in each segment and channel.

Sales training will address a more complex sales environment

"The salesperson has to acquire expert knowledge, and has to translate that knowledge into a language customers are able to understand."

—Training manager, Bayerische Vereinsbank
(Germany)

Face-to-face communication skills will remain a primary focus in sales training. Consultative selling, for example, requires skillful listening and questioning. Self-led sales teams and team selling will continue to increase in importance and so will team skills: orchestration of individuals, team dynamics, and leadership. Training in teams will prepare members for their individual sales roles.

Allen & Hanbury's: Selling against Competition

Over the past decades, the pharmaceutical industry in the United Kingdom has become far more competitive, and the battle for market share has become more intense. In addition, the industry has become a massive business.

Tighter government controls and other policy changes in the National Health Service have made hospitals and individual clinic practices more price-sensitive and more demanding in their expectations of the pharmaceutical companies that sell to them. These customers want their time to be used effectively; they expect sales reps to be knowledgeable, to solve problems, and to be flexible in making decisions and responding to their needs. As a result, pharmaceutical companies have to be sharper about finding competitive advantages. In this business environment, the role of training is essential.

"Training is very focused on the job salespeople are expected to do," says Allen & Hanbury's training manager. The firm's salespeople go through a 12-week training program. The first five weeks consist of training in the field and in the head office. Selling skills training helps them obtain product knowledge and, using role playing, learn to focus more on the customer's needs. The next six weeks are spent in the field calling on customers, supported by a field trainer. The final week is spent in the office, training to refresh their knowledge and skills.

When all the training is complete, targets for competence levels are set for each rep at three- and six-month intervals. Individual performance is tracked through their trainers, and additional training and product refreshers are given to address shortfalls. To ensure that the new skills are practiced and applied, each representative creates a learning contract that identifies his or her goals and an action plan to achieve them.

Coaching plays a vital role in guiding the salespeople. Regional managers assess the representatives' performance in all areas through field observation—approximately 20 days spent with each rep in the field per year. They observe the use of skills and knowledge in action and provide feedback. The field trainers do the same, typically spending from 8 to 16 days per year with each rep. In addition, the reps attend local training seminars run by field trainers and use videos to coach on selling skills. "It is absolutely essential to make those skills second nature," says the vice president for sales.

(continued)

Allen & Hanbury's: Selling against Competition (concluded)

In the future, salespeople will receive more general business train-ing. "We want our representatives to understand why the customers behave the way they do, as businesspeople. We also want to give them the ability and confidence to have more autonomy, so they can make more business decisions locally," says the training manager.

The importance of product knowledge training will increase. Sales-training will emphasize the wider range of knowledge required for consultative selling. General business knowledge and business management skills will increase in importance as salespeople run their territories in a more entrepreneurial manner.

Sales training will be more practical

"As a sales organization, we need to know how a customer makes decisions and how we provide value in that context. As a training organization, we need to prepare our sales and service organizations to deliver that."

—Vice president, Xerox Corporation
(United States)

Training will reflect the changes in the customers' needs and expec-tations and in the organization's sales strategy. It will also emphasize selling to more senior management. "They must be able to discuss the relationship of our products to business issues with senior exec-utives," asserted a vice president, Hewlett-Packard (United States).

Sales training will be evaluated more methodically

"Companies must systematically identify training needs, build content into training programs based on job information, and evaluate training in terms of the objectives for which it was designed. Only then will the field of training arid development cease to be an art form that is dependent on the persuasive-ness of the advocates, and instead be a science that is repeatable by others.[2]

---

[2] N. Wexley and G. P. Latham, *Developing and Training Human Resources in Organizations* (New York: HarperCollins, 1991), p. 91.

Virtually every training professional recognizes that systematic evaluation of training is a crucial need. The measurement of training will be used to focus on process improvement, not just on justifying the training—on improving, not just proving.[3]

Sales training will be more specific to the needs of the individual

"The key thing is to ensure that the salespeople want to do something about their particular development area, so they are keen to progress. If the training is dovetailed to suit those requirements, you will succeed."

—Sales manager, Allen & Hanbury's
(United Kingdom)

Identification of an individual's strengths and weaknesses is a key to the success of training.

There will be more just-in-time training

"We are incorporating the just-in-time concept—for example, data on customer satisfaction—into our training department to find ways to get information to salespeople at the moment they need it."

—Training manager, Northwestern Mutual Life Insurance Company
(United States)

---

[3]D. L. Kirkpatrick, "Techniques for Evaluating Training Programs," *Training Director's Journal* (November 1959). One classic model for evaluating training is Kirkpatrick's four levels of validation:

Level I validation answers the question, "How did participants feel about the training?" Interviews or questionnaires can be used to answer this question. The results reveal what may be done to improve seminar procedures or content to make the training more valuable to participants.

Level II validation answers the question, "Were learning objectives met?" Tests or work simulations can help answer this question.

Level III validation answers the "transfer of training" question; in other words, "Are salespeople demonstrating appropriate use of competencies on the job?" Behavioral observations, interviews, or customer satisfaction results can shed some light on this.

Level IV validation answers the question, "Are the objectives of training being met?" Revenues or customer satisfaction results again may answer this question.

Just-in-time training means providing training when it is needed. It can also mean using information immediately to make adjustments in training programs.

Sales training will be a systematic process

"If you want to accomplish a culture change, it is critical to train the sales managers first. That way, the managers can be teachers and leaders. Otherwise, they are followers, and are forced to be reactive."

—Sales manager, Xerox Corporation
(United States)

Instead of a series of discrete training events, sales training will be a more continuous learning process that addresses the needs of sales-people as they progress along a career path. It will be more systematic in its implementation, including more organized reinforcement, follow-up, and coaching to ensure that what is learned in training is actually incorporated into each salesperson's daily activities.

Sales training will include managers more frequently, and at an earlier stage, to ensure that they know what their salespeople are learning. Coaching training for sales managers and others will prepare them to be teachers and leaders who provide better on-the-job feedback to salespeople. In some companies, such as Océ (France), managers are actually involved in the delivery of sales training. It refreshes their basic skills and works to improve the camaraderie within the sales team.

Sales training will be delivered in innovative ways

"A one-way, lecture-type training program is not effective. Training participation is important."

—Training manager, Sony Corporation
(Japan)

As teleconferencing technology improves and expands, companies will find it easier to provide "distance learning." This will expand the concept of the virtual classroom and provide a less expensive alternative to traditional seminar-based programs that may involve substantial travel cost. Interactive computer software, delivered via CD-ROM and CDI (interactive CD), is another technology alternative.

Sales training will include nontraditional populations

"Training will be done by the same company for the buyer and for the salesperson."

—Training manager, Ordo
(France)

Buyers and sellers will participate in training together, as partners.

Sales training will be used to reinforce global strategies

"We must train to handle future challenges, not train to handle what has already happened."

—Salesperson, Rank Xerox
(Sweden)

As companies become global in scope, training will be used to create a sales culture within a worldwide organization that is based on a common set of values and skills, yet responsive to the demands of local markets.

CONCLUSION

"The acquisition of knowledge is a journey, not a destination."

—Vice president, Northwestern Mutual Life Insurance Company
(United States)

With the profound changes taking place in today's market, every organization has to be more nimble than ever. Each sales director must constantly reevaluate the sales strategy in relation to the changes taking place. But it's not enough to simply adjust the strategy; it is more important than ever that the entire organization be prepared to execute the strategy effectively and reliably.

It is critical that those responsible for designing and implementing training have the information and support they need to make those changes faster and more effectively.

Everyone in the sales organization should be focused on ensuring that there is a tight connection between sales training and sales strategy—that the sales training your organization provides is truly strategic sales training.

BEST PRACTICES AND GUIDING PRINCIPLES

- Use sales training as a tool to translate strategy into focused activity. A company's success in doing this depends largely on designing training programs that respond to the question, "What should salespeople do differently to implement the sales strategy?"
- Use the organization's Customer Relationship Process to identify the training needs of salespeople and sales team members.
- Sales executives should never assume that they are providing enough information to the training staff to guide decisions about training program development. This understanding has to be confirmed. An effective way to do this is to create a dialogue among sales executives and training professionals. This dialogue should focus on:

  How customers, competitors, products, and services are changing

  How sales strategies are changing to keep up with changes in the market

  The new roles salespeople will play to implement a sales strategy

  How salespeople should sell differently

- To ensure that today's sales training supports today's strategy, look at the training program development process. Use the concepts of process management to find ways to shorten the time span between when the sales strategy is dictated and when training is implemented.
- Follow the model for strategic sales training outlined in this chapter. The only way to ensure that the training at the end of the path is consistent with the sales strategy is to ensure that all the steps in the process are executed well.
- Have a plan for systematic sales training for salespeople and sales managers in the organization. For example, whenever possible, train sales managers first, maintain managers' involvement in training salespeople, and ensure that salespeople are fully prepared; this means they must know what is expected of them and what the training will accomplish.
- Sales training is a process. As in any process, put measurements in place to ensure that each step is executed effectively.

  Measurement at a number of points is an effective way to diagnose causes for less-than-desired outcomes, identify improvement opportunities, and assess particular competencies that should be the focus of follow-up training and reinforcement.

- Follow-up and reinforcement are absolutely critical. Salespeople will learn new behaviors in training; however, there are sometimes several weeks of "turbulence" back on the job while salespeople unlearn old habits and integrate new ones. Feedback, reinforcement, and assessment of strengths and weaknesses are ways to ensure that the training investment is made profitable. Follow-up and reinforcement are areas where many organizations—even some of the best sales organizations—can make tremendous gains.

- Ensure that the new behaviors learned in training are consistent with the organizational environment. For instance, if compensation or other reward plans are inconsistent with new behaviors, the training won't work.

- Look carefully at the trends in sales training. Determine those that are relevant to the organization.

Chapter Twelve

Strategic Sales Coaching

"One of the most important roles in our organization is sales coaching. It is like being a conductor of a symphonic orchestra—without it, there would be nothing played at all."

—District sales manager, Rank Xerox
(Sweden)

- What is strategic sales coaching?
- How can collaborative coaching enhance the performance of salespeople?
- What is meant by the "generation gap" between salespeople and sales coaches?
- What roles do effective sales managers fulfill?
- What are the barriers to effective sales coaching? How can sales managers overcome them?
- What are some important elements of sales coaching training?

Across industries, markets, and cultures—in North America, Europe, and Japan—there is a clear and unanimous vision of the profile of the ideal sales coach and the mission of sales coaching. There is also an astounding degree of consensus among salespeople, sales managers, and sales executives about the potential power of sales coaching: They agree that sales coaching is one of the most significant opportunities available to an organization to influence the performance of salespeople.

Yet in many sales organizations, there is a significant gap between the vision of sales coaching and the reality. Why? Because there has been no commitment to support sales coaching and to redefine the role of the field sales manager for today's business environment. In fact, sales managers at even the most successful sales organizations are missing important coaching opportunities—opportunities to translate sales strategy into everyday actions that can be carried out by the people they lead.

The leading sales organizations are constantly challenging themselves with the following questions:

- What is the profile of an ideal sales coach?
- What is the gap between the ideal and the reality?
- Why does the gap exist?

CRITICAL FACTORS IN COACHING

"On a scale of 1 to 10, sales coaching ranks an 11. It is extremely important."

—Field sales manager, Allen & Hanbury's
(United Kingdom)

Coaching guides the development of a salesperson through one-on-one feedback and encouragement. Explained a vice president from Biscuiterie Nantaise (France), "Coaching can increase a salesperson's knowledge and set up the conditions necessary for self-development. It increases the self-confidence of the salesperson and creates a dialogue about performance."

According to salespeople, the best coaches don't tell salespeople what to do; they collaborate with them to achieve mutually agreed-upon goals. They use their coaching skills—combined with knowledge of the customer and the behind-the-scenes workings of the sales organization—to motivate their salespeople to seek continual improvement in their abilities. As a sales manager from American Airlines (United States) put it, "One of the factors that keeps us at the forefront of the industry is that managers are very communicative with individuals in counseling them, coaching them, and working with them." A vice president for France's Ordo predicted that in five years the top salespeople in his company will be the ones who benefited from effective sales coaching.

Coaching is a critical tool for sales organizations that are committed to building long-term customer relationships. To be effective in today's business environment, sales coaching must be

- *Collaborative*—a joint, ongoing process in which sales managers and team members work together to achieve both short- and long-term sales goals.

- *Contemporary*—shaped by the needs of *today's* demanding customer and competitive marketplace as well as by the salesperson's individual development requirements.

COLLABORATIVE COACHING: FAREWELL TO THE AUTOCRATIC MANAGER

"The best sales coaches are respected by their people for their wide perspective."

—Sales manager, Sony Corporation
(Japan)

Sales coaching is evolving in leading sales organizations, moving away from the traditional authoritarian patterns of manager-subordinate relationships and toward a more collaborative effort based on mutual respect and trust in which the salesperson and coach work together to achieve a common goal.

What does this look like in everyday life? Rather than *direct* the salesperson's actions, the best coaches help salespeople find their own solutions. "They adopt a counseling approach, letting the person talk and trying to redirect the discussion if they feel it's necessary," commented a sales manager from Iron Trades Insurance Group (United Kingdom). "The ideas that people take on board are ideas they feel are their own."

Effective sales managers collaborate with sales team members rather than "manage" in the traditional sense of the word. They use their authority wisely, encouraging team members to think independently. "A good coach gets you thinking about certain things, even if he or she knows the answers to the questions," observed a salesperson from Hewlett-Packard Company (United States). Not only do they resist dictating, they also resist taking over. The best coaches resist the temptation to step in and fix their salespeople's problems. They weigh the advantages of taking risks and learning-by-doing against the potential for lost time and opportunity.

The best coaches lead by example, rather than by fiat, according to both sales managers and salespeople. "Merely demanding results will not be accepted by subordinates," commented a vice president from Sony Corporation (Japan). A salesperson from Matra Communications (France) remarked, "I prefer the human contact, not just a

---

Sales Coaching

A sequence of conversations and activities that provides ongoing feedback and encouragement to a salesperson or sales team member with the goal of improving that person's performance.

Strategic Sales Coaching

The use of sales coaching to achieve a sales strategy in a systematic way.

---

boss-employee relationship." Said another from 3M (United Kingdom), "Sales coaches are there to help and not to direct."

The evolution of a collaborative model for sales coaching may be a partial consequence of the organizational changes wrought by the recent worldwide recessions. Many salespeople have stayed longer in their positions than they might have in the past, because of lack of opportunities elsewhere. As a result, many sales managers supervise sales representatives who are more educated and experienced than ever before. A collaborative approach to solving problems is one way to draw on the strengths of their resources. "With flatter organizations and changes in corporate culture, the most effective role for a sales manager is that of a coach, not an autocrat," observed a vice president from Xerox Corporation (United States). This is not to say that the collaborative approach doesn't benefit new salespeople; in fact, although they lack experience, there's a good chance they started their careers in less hierarchical organizations and aren't accustomed to the traditional authority structures.

The collaborative approach is not only a result of economics. Coincidentally, sales organizations have found that the partnerships they're consciously forming with their customers are increasingly mirrored in the relationships within their own walls, including the sales manager–salesperson relationship. This development, in fact, is encouraged: "Sales managers have to look at their salespeople as customers and think about their needs," observed a vice president from Scott Paper Company (United States). "You should probe to clarify and understand. Apply the customer needs model to your own salespeople."

In the best cases, sales coaching is a two-way exchange. In one instance, the coach may provide the salesperson with pointers on handling a customer's skepticism. In another, the salesperson may comment on how the coach interacted with the customer during a joint sales call.

Sales coaching focuses on sales behaviors that directly affect results. The effective coach looks for behaviors that demonstrate the salesperson's knowledge of the organization's products and services, mastery of the Customer Relationship Process, facility with critical selling skills (e.g., face-to-face selling, account planning, and negotiation), and knowledge of the customer's needs. A structured process can help to keep this focus.

A sales manager from Allen & Hanbury's (United Kingdom) describes how the sales coaching process works in that organization:

> Each individual salesperson is assessed to see where skills must be improved to bring about an improvement in overall performance. There is a plan for each individual which is referred to, documented, and reviewed every time there is contact with that individual on a field visit.

As the Allen & Hanbury's example illustrates, sales coaching consists of two distinct, ongoing activities:

1. *Diagnosis,* in which the coach and salesperson jointly identify those behaviors that can be improved to better achieve the salesperson's targets and the organization's sales strategy. This may involve observing, reviewing revenue and customer feedback data, and gathering input from others in the company.

2. *Action planning,* in which the coach and salesperson jointly set goals based on their diagnosis. In action planning, the coach guides the process by which the salesperson finds solutions and creates plans to support short- and long-term changes that will lead to improved performance.

CONTEMPORARY COACHING: OVERCOMING THE GENERATION GAP

"My goal is to have every one of our salespeople developing, growing, and improving every day."

—Vice president, Scott Paper Company
(United States)

A major challenge sales managers face in being effective coaches is addressing the needs of more sophisticated, better educated salespeople. As demonstrated earlier, many salespeople are staying in their jobs longer than in previous years. In addition, most top sales organizations have changed their hiring criteria for salespeople. "We will be adding levels of sophistication to the salesperson's job, looking for a higher level of individual to fill it," said a vice president from Hewlett-Packard Company (United States). "That will mean the sales manager's job will be more demanding, as a manager of more sophisticated resources."

Another challenge sales managers face is keeping themselves up to date about selling strategies that are effective in today's rapidly changing marketplace. Sales managers who were once sales representatives will find that their natural inclination is to coach people in the strategies that worked for them in the past. The problem is that the strategies that worked in previous years often do not work in today's marketplace. Customer expectations have changed—in some cases so radically that managers should question whether customers' current needs bear any resemblance to their needs when the managers themselves were salespeople. Much of their experience may, in fact, be irrelevant.

"In the past, the 'supersellers' climbed to the sales management level," commented a vice president from Bekaert (Belgium). "However, they are not adapted to today's selling strategy, and there is definitely a generation gap."

Salespeople need coaching that helps them meet the high expectations of *today's* customers. Customers want to work with a salesperson who is a strategic orchestrator, business consultant, and long-term ally—someone interested in the success of the customer's business as a whole, not just in selling a product. Yet the coaching many salespeople receive is too basic, and too infrequent, to help them develop, sell, and deliver the complex solutions their customers need and want.

In the role of strategist, the sales manager also develops and/or utilizes appropriate structures and systems to recruit sales personnel, create sales assignments, reward performance, pursue new business, and forecast and track revenue. He or she builds alliances throughout the organization; knows when to involve internal people or outside resources to solve problems; and supplies salespeople with the sales support, tools, and technology they need.

The Power of "Transformational Leadership"

"No orders, no money." Those words, imprinted on a sign above a sales manager's desk in a commission-oriented organization, represent the reward-for-results approach often used to prod salespeople to perform. Although this approach is effective in many organizations, Marvin Jolson, Alan Dubinsky, and their colleagues, writing in the *Sloan Management Review,* believe there's more to inspiring sales success than simply dangling a cash carrot.[1] They suggest that the most successful sales organizations are headed by executives who employ a combination of *transactional* and *transformational* leadership styles with a heavy emphasis on the transformational. Not surprisingly, many of the attributes of the transformational leadership style come into play in the sales manager's role as coach.

Transactional leaders motivate staff with bonuses and commissions and subscribe to a laissez-faire style of management. They establish specific targets for their people and then step back, intervening only if salespeople have trouble meeting them.

While independent self-starters may thrive under transactional leadership, inexperienced or less confident salespeople frequently perish without more guidance and feedback. Transformational leaders provide a more nurturing and, in most cases, motivational environment. This breed of leader is characterized by his or her charisma and ability to provide intellectual stimulation and individualized consideration.

Transformational managers' *charisma* inspires admiration, respect, and trust in team members. Just as important, these managers lead by example, continually modeling and reinforcing desirable attitudes and behaviors. They empower their good performers, and they exhibit genuine confidence in their salespeople.

Intellectual stimulation is a tool transformational managers use to help their people overcome sales barriers and achieve new levels of performance. It takes many forms, from encouraging creativity in solving old problems to introducing innovative prospecting and selling strategies and promoting ongoing education and learning.

Through *individualized consideration,* the transformational manager works hard to create strong, one-on-one relationships with each sales team member. That means focusing less on tasks, policies, administrative matters, or decision making and more on spending time with salespeople in their territories, holding private coaching sessions, analyzing call reports, and extending warmth and understanding.

(continued)

> *The Power of "Transformational Leadership" (concluded)*
>
> What does it take to foster the transformational style of leadership? According to Jolson and his colleagues, the first step is to recruit sales personnel with transformational qualities and characteristics. Look for innovative and creative problem solvers and risk takers. An entrepreneurial spirit, courage, and strong personal convictions are also important. Second, provide training and development. "Because all individuals possess transformational skills to some degree," say the authors, "even minimal levels of these skills can be enhanced through training."
>
> [1]Marvin A. Jolson, Alan J. Dubinsky, et al., "Transforming the Sales Force with Leadership," *Sloan Management Review* (Spring 1993), pp. 95–106..

THREE ROLES OF THE EFFECTIVE SALES MANAGER

Knowledge of today's marketplace not only enables sales managers to guide salespeople to customer-driven solutions; it helps them serve as effective role models for their people. It also earns the sales team's respect—a key ingredient, given *salespeople's* increasing sophistication and education.

AchieveGlobal's research indicates that top-performing sales managers fulfill three key roles (see Figure 12-1). As judged by their subordinates, colleagues, and managers, and by their track record for meeting or exceeding quotas, highly effective sales managers perform the actions associated with the following three roles better than do their less effective colleagues:

- As a *strategist,* the sales manager utilizes knowledge of the organization's sales strategy and industry and market trends, needs, and perceptions to develop team strategies and goals that reflect a balance between attaining financial goals and satisfying customers. The sales manager ensures that others understand these goals; obtains commitment from salespeople to achieve them; and modifies strategies, processes, and activities based on the team's success at building lasting customer relationships.

- As *a communicator,* the sales manager organizes and uses information effectively, obtaining it from and sharing it with the sales team, management, and other groups. He or she possesses the interpersonal skills to seek a clear understanding of all communications, clarify expectations, and resolve conflict. The

FIGURE 12-1
The Effective Sales Manager

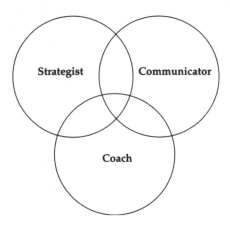

sales manager also utilizes basic and advanced selling, presentation, and negotiating skills to support salespeople in selling to accounts. He or she ensures that meeting time is used productively, maintains complete and accurate records, and gathers and uses feedback to improve customer relationships and internal processes.

- As a *coach*, the sales manager establishes an environment for performance improvement. He or she does this by maintaining good rapport with the sales team and fostering open communication, collaboration, creativity, initiative, and appropriate risk taking. The sales manager encourages team members to seek information and resources to enhance their success with customers. He or she models professional attitudes and behaviors. The sales manager demonstrates awareness of individual differences among team members, helps salespeople establish clear priorities, and gives appropriate rewards and recognition.

In the role of coach, the sales manager provides each salesperson with specific feedback on strengths and weaknesses. He or she works with each person to create and implement a developmental plan to improve performance, which includes providing ongoing training and coaching in selling skills, sales strategy, and product and market knowledge.

BREAKING DOWN THE BARRIERS

"For best results, coaching must be a structured process. It cannot be left up to the individual manager."

—Sales Vice President

Pressured by short-term needs to achieve revenue targets and performance goals, many sales organizations have difficulty putting a value on the long-term benefits of sales coaching. Managers and salespeople naturally focus on the activities for which they are directly rewarded and compensated.

Sales coaching is an essential factor in ensuring progress toward long-term goals that is consistent with the sales strategy, day by day in front of customers. Effective coaching is a steady process designed to improve salespeople's selling skills and abilities progressively over the months and years of their careers in sales. It builds on the knowledge, skills, and attitudes that salespeople learn in sales training. Sales coaching also draws on a powerful existing resource: the experienced base of sales managers.

In organizations where coaching is supported by sales vice presidents and directors, it is a powerful tool for translating a sales strategy into everyday action. For the vast majority of other organizations, however, coaching's benefits remain unrealized.

Senior executives can play a key role in tapping the tremendous power of sales coaching. To do this, they need to understand how sales coaching can contribute to the overall sales strategy and how they will support the coaching effort. To ensure the success of the coaching process, senior executives need to change the ways that sales managers are selected, trained, motivated, and compensated.

In organizations where sales coaching is effective, the following actions are taken:

1. Sales managers understand that sales coaching is a priority because it supports the organization's strategy for winning and keeping customers over the long and short term. There are many ways to do this, and some of them very simple. For example, sales managers from Allen & Hanbury's have "learning contracts" with their manager, who periodically observes the managers at work with their salespeople. Sales managers are also required to send copies of their field visit reports to the national sales manager.

2. *Everyone has the same expectations of sales coaching.*
AchieveGlobal's research indicated a wide variation among
what sales managers, salespeople, senior sales executives,
and even trainers believed a realistic coaching plan to be.
With an agreed-upon definition, such as the one provided at
the beginning of this chapter, sales coaches and salespeople
can more easily set priorities and establish an effective game
plan for improving the salesperson's interactions with customers. In addition, others in the organization, such as senior
management and training decision makers, will know how
to channel their resources to support each salesperson's performance improvement.

3. *Coaches are trained according to their organization's definition of
coaching.* A definition that is understood and accepted
throughout the sales organization will provide clear direction toward the training that coaches need to be effective.
The resulting training strategy can alleviate conflicting perceptions about how much coaching is occurring or about
whether the coaching is actually useful to salespeople in
their interactions with customers.

4. *All salespeople receive coaching.* Fast-changing market dynamics and new sales objectives make it imperative to provide
coaching to all salespeople, not just to the new, inexperienced, or poor performers. Even if the sales manager cannot
provide the coaching, he or she should select and train someone who can, be it another salesperson or someone hired
specifically for the job.

5. *Coaches receive continuing education in market, industry, and
product knowledge so they can apply leading-edge information and
thinking to the situations their salespeople encounter in today's
selling environment.* Of particular importance is that coaches
understand the realities of today's customers and are able to
guide their people in addressing them.

6. *Coaches are involved in setting objectives for training programs.*
By turning to the coaches to help set objectives for training
programs and even participate in their delivery, organizations can ensure that they align their sales training with current sales strategy. Coaches, in turn, will be able to build on
this training in their one-on-one coaching sessions with
salespeople.

7. *Others in the organization also coach.* Sales managers are the
   obvious choice to coach salespeople on a consistent basis, but
   others, such as senior sales executives and business managers, can provide key input into how best to meet customer
   needs. Dividing up the responsibility in this way also enables
   the organization to provide its salespeople with critical support without incurring additional cost or taking sales managers away from other activities that they need to address.
   As more organizations work in sales teams, coaching from
   team members is increasing.

TRAINING FOR COLLABORATIVE AND CONTEMPORARY COACHING

Given the complexity of today's selling challenges, it is clear that
sales coaches need more than an inborn talent for being "good with
people." Training in interpersonal communication skills that enable
them to develop salespeople's ability to achieve the organization's
financial and customer satisfaction goals is essential. Too often, however, the sales coach's own experience is thought to be an adequate
source of sales wisdom, improvement strategies, and motivation.

Coaching Guidance from Several Sources

Salespeople both welcome and value coaching from their peers,
training managers, business managers, technical experts, and even
customers. "Your peers are your best coaches," said a salesperson
from Northwestern Mutual Life Insurance Company (United States).
"They are people you can trust, that know what you're doing." A
salesperson from Boehme (Germany) commented, "Feedback comes
from customers in the form of compliments, contracts, and sales."

"In the future," commented a vice president from Océ (The
Netherlands), "not all coaching will be done by sales managers;
some will be provided by technical specialists." A sales manager at
Fuji Xerox (Japan) agrees: "Sales organizations will have to stretch
themselves and explore new options."

The belief that sales coaching will happen naturally may explain why even some of today's top sales organizations have not implemented a training plan in specific sales coaching skills. In some organizations the curriculum comprises a combination of management instruction and advanced sales training.

Not surprisingly, these organizations are not satisfied with their efforts to prepare sales managers for their coaching responsibilities. In fact, improving the competence of sales coaches appeared at the top of the list of most companies' strategies for ensuring their salespeople's success in the next 5 to 10 years.

Some organizations have taken steps to realize their beliefs about the importance of coaching. These actions range from hiring a development manager for their sales organizations, to implementing training in sales coaching, to spelling out a schedule for their sales managers' coaching activities.

The principle underlying all these actions is a commitment to ensure that their sales managers accomplish the following:

1. Establish a developmental climate based on collaboration and action in which continuous performance improvement is both encouraged and rewarded.
2. Identify for salespeople the desired performance outcomes that will achieve the organization's short- *and* long-term goals.
3. Create individual performance improvement plans that address the unique developmental needs of each sales team member.
4. Encourage and reward salespeople who achieve their developmental goals.

A comprehensive training strategy for sales coaches should include the same training that the salespeople experience. Through coaching training, sales managers come to understand not only the skills their salespeople have mastered in their own training but how to use the coaching process to build those skills and support the organization's overall sales strategy. They acquire a distinct set of interpersonal skills to diagnose each salesperson's skill development needs and to create plans to address them. They also learn how to *observe* sales interactions, not just participate in them.

Without adequate and appropriate training for sales managers, sales coaching will remain a disorganized and underutilized tool.

The Coaching Payoff: Win. Wrigley Jr. Company

Coaching can increase an organization's success with customers, protect its sales training investments, and unify the sales force around common strategic and developmental objectives.

The Win. Wrigley Jr. Company (United States), for example, has made coaching an integral part of its sales force training strategy. The chewing gum manufacturer started by creating task forces to define what, exactly, its salespeople and regional sales managers needed to do to ensure salespeople's success with customers. The task forces, which included managers and sales representatives from across the country, established benchmarks for salesperson performance to enable the company's regional managers to know exactly what areas to coach on—and when, why, and how.

"At one time, when our sales representatives left our training sessions and went out in the field, we had no idea how the skills were being reinforced," says one of Wrigley's division managers. "Depending on the skills and experience of the manager, one representative might receive coaching in setting up displays, another on improving selling skills. Now we have a development process based on benchmarks for successive stages in a salesperson's career.

"The process includes training the salespeople and the sales managers in critical skills, so the sales managers are able to identify their salespeople's strengths and weaknesses. As a result, our managers should be able to assess which stage their people are in and what skills they should have mastered. They'll also have the confidence, knowledge, and tools to coach their people effectively."

Hurlburt acknowledges the strategy would not be working as well if it were not for senior management involvement. "If senior management simply went along with a plan like this and didn't get involved, then our field people would think that *their* participation at less than 100 percent was also acceptable."[2] As these actions demonstrate, Win. Wrigley Jr. believes effective sales coaching is one vehicle that enables them to maximize their sales organization's performance with customers.

---

[2]AchieveGlobal, *Sales Coaching: The Key to Leading a High Performance Sales Team* (1994).

With training, sales coaching is far more likely to yield positive re-sults—for both the selling organization and its customers.

CONCLUSION

"Coaching rekindles the fire."

—Sales manager, Ordo (France)

Removing the obstacles to effective sales coaching isn't easy. If it were, every organization would already provide salespeople with the coaching they need. But in today's marketplace, coaching is no longer a "wish-list item." It's crucial, not only for poor performers but also for the most effective. A vice president from Iron Trades Insurance Group (United Kingdom) feels that "unless sales coaching is done, and done well throughout the sales organization, then our high standards will drop."

Organizations that implement a sales-coaching process are far more able to achieve both their profitability and their customer-satisfaction goals. In fact, they gain a substantial competitive advantage because they have made a commitment to ensuring that their salespeople's daily selling behaviors lead to mutually beneficial business relationships with customers.

BEST PRACTICES AND GUIDING PRINCIPLES

- Start with a demonstrated commitment to sales coaching by creating a developmental climate that fosters:

  Collaboration, action, and continuous improvement

  Shared understanding of salesperson performance outcomes that will achieve both short- and long-term goals

  Development of individual performance improvement plans

  Behavior change

- Ensure that senior executives and all members of the sales organization can answer these questions accurately:

What are the sales organization's expectations for sales coaching? How will it work?

How can sales coaching contribute to the organization's strategy for winning and keeping customers over the short and long term?

- Have senior executives provide visible support for sales coaching.
- Ensure that sales coaching training is consistent with the company's definition of coaching.
- Put a structured approach to sales coaching in place. Don't leave the approach completely up to the individual.
- Involve both sales managers and salespeople in the design and implementation of sales-coaching programs, as well as sales staff development programs.
- Provide sales coaching to every salesperson, regardless of tenure or performance level. Tailor sales coaching to individual salespeople.
- Ensure that all sales coaches:

  Receive continuing education to improve market, industry, and product knowledge.

  Maintain involvement in sales staff developmental programs.

- Seek out and develop sales managers who:

  Have a broad scope of knowledge.

  Are able to provide inspiration and intellectual stimulation.

  Are considerate of individuals' needs.

- Utilize a variety of people, such as peers and technical experts, in sales coaching, not just the salesperson's manager.
- Focus sales coaching on knowledge and skills that support the sales strategy. The foundation should be:

  Knowledge of the organization's products and services.

  Customers' needs and expectations.

  Mastery of the company's Customer Relationship Process.

- Sales coaching should be:

  Collaborative—a two-way exchange involving the input of both salespeople and sales managers.

  Contemporary—grounded in the needs of today's, not yesterday's, markets and customers.

- Sales coaching training should focus on interpersonal skills, diagnosis and action-planning, and sales call observation. Sales managers should also receive continuing education to maintain current market, industry, and product knowledge.
- Sales managers should collect sufficient information about the performance of salespeople to be able to diagnose improvement needs and work with the salesperson to develop an action plan.
- Sales managers should understand the importance of fulfilling the three roles (strategist, communicator, and coach) as well as the characteristics of each.
- Sales managers should treat salespeople as customers (for instance, continually think about their needs).

The Next Wave

"Business as usual is the fastest route to extinction. That doesn't mean you throw out everything you know; but it does mean that you keep looking out ahead for what's on the horizon and move fast when things inevitably change."

There was a time when companies made products or provided services and salespeople sold them. Simple. Then, sometime in the 1980s, the "if we build it, they will buy" model stopped working. Increasingly aggressive competitors, leapfrogging advances in technology, more complex sales and sales cycles, matrixed organizations, pressure from buyers who are themselves under pressure from *their* customers, as well as a grab bag of other challenges are the day-to-day reality of selling today. Whether they sell biscuits or digital networks, salespeople are looking for new ways to win—and maintain—market share.

The struggle is forcing sales organizations to move more quickly, be more innovative, and jettison old habits and assumptions about business relationships. How those relationships are built and maintained and who is involved continues to evolve. And, while consultative selling emerges as a clear winner in building true partnerships, the tools, methods, and processes that support the consultative role are continually being reexamined and challenged.

As organizations are reengineered, so, too, is the sales function. More systematized, repeatable outcomes, with ISO-9000-type certifications, are all part of this trend. Benchmarking provides lessons from industry leaders. Training, retention recognition, and coaching become even more important in an environment of team selling and self-directed sales teams. Sales teams become more empowered, with sales managers taking on new roles, often with little direct sales contact. Customer needs move front and center as the driving force for the organization. Specific product features and benefits take a back seat to the partnering nature of the relationship. What's on the horizon for sales? Things change quickly but forward-thinking sales organizations are looking at these issues:

- *Knowledge management.* Today's technology allows an organization to do much more than simply track data and crunch numbers. Businesses are using enterprisewide "knowledge systems" to capture, store, and retrieve the collective brainpower of the organization. Knowledge management systems have become the key to deepening customer relationships, using information, history, precedents, and prior experience to refine the relationship and better meet customer needs. Two significant challenges remain, however. The first is ensuring that the newly available knowledge is *used and applied.* Getting the knowledge from those who have it to those who need it to make intelligent business decisions requires a finely tuned combination of people, processes, and technology. The second challenge involves changing the culture to place a higher value on the contribution, sharing, and utilization of knowledge rather than on the knowledge itself. This is a major shift in the way an organization determines hiring profiles, compensation, rewards, and recognition.

- *New markets with new rules.* Both emerging markets (Eastern Europe, for example) and recovering markets (South Africa and Asia) require new techniques. Prior knowledge, experience, and a clear understanding of the state of business in each country is key to succeeding. In emerging markets, pent-up demand created an era of "order-taking." As demand is filled, professional sales techniques are required to build customer loyalty. However, the skills do not exist and are a challenge to develop in countries where there is little traditional of a customer-focused orientation. In recovering markets, old habits and traditions may reemerge that clash with the marketplace needs, while at the same time, cutting-edge organizations are emerging with different decision styles. Awareness of the diversity and unique situation, and infinite flexibility of salespeople and sales organizations is critical. The concept of the business consultant who can sell an entire solution takes on even more meaning, with the need to link and support solutions to the actual economic growth or recovery.

- *Globalization.* Emerging and recovering markets are just one prong of a globalization common to all industries. The Internet has made Marshal McLuhan's Global Village a real place where trade is in the universal language of "business." A salesperson talking to a customer in South Carolina may find that the solution is influenced by manufacturing decisions in France or distribution issues in India. Cross-cultural awareness and knowledge of the interrelated nature of the business is critical to add value to a business relationship.

- *One-to-one marketing.* Technology makes it possible to target direct marketing to the needs of individual customers. Mass customization can provide individualized products and services. Customers have direct access to organizations through telephone, mail, and Internet. The challenge for the sales organization is to leverage this high contact, unique marketing opportunity into more than order filling. At certain levels, the customer will control the sale and there will be no salesperson involvement. (See "High-tech versus high-touch.")

- *Complexity of organizations, products, and services.* Layers of influence, decision making, and contacts in the buyer's organization complicate the relationship process. Multiple resources within the seller's organization need to be coordinated. Complex products and services challenge the salesperson's ability to present the right solution for customer needs. No one person can know enough about their organization's capabilities to be the expert. The salesperson is increasingly a strategic orchestrator of internal and external resources.

- *High-tech versus high-touch.* High-tech selling—Internet, video kiosks, telephone sales, TV—will become more prevalent. Already making inroads in travel, automobile, auctions, computers, and software, cyber sales remain an unknown in terms of their impact on business-to-business sales. The salesperson's strength will be in the higher-level, more complex sale in which business issues are the defining factors—not price, features, or delivery. High-touch will, in fact, be even more important in these complex, longer cycle sales.

- *Strength in numbers.* As smaller businesses face competition from industry giants, they are banding together to be more competitive in their market. Hardware stores, for example, have formed single-source buying units with multiple members across the country. Buying groups are better able to negotiate price and terms—good for them but often a challenge for the sales organization. The challenge is often addressed through alliances with key customers to build profit through volume and add value through customized services.

- *Better equipped virtual offices.* Technology, reorganizations, and budgets are continuing the trend to the non-office-based salesperson. More reliable and powerful cell phones, feature-rich laptops, personal digital assistants, voice mail, e-mail, networked databases, and more sophisticated project management software make it possible for the salesperson to "office" almost anywhere, yet have more access to knowledge about products, customers, and the market than ever before.

- *More authority, less management.* Self-directed sales teams have more authority to make decisions and, as a result, react to customer needs more quickly. Sales managers may have responsibility for multiple teams in widely separated locations. The challenge is to maintain coaching and performance support in an environment where face-to-face contact between salesperson and sales manager may be rare. In order to maintain the informal communication and relationships that build teams, some companies have mandated a "fly-in Friday" when all members of a team are at the "office"—not for a formal meeting but simply to spend time as a group.

The next few years will see more changes in sales organizations and selling than have taken place in the last 10. Success and growth in the profession belong to those people who are ready for the changes. Flexibility—in skills, attitude, and know-how—will help you ride the next wave.

Appendix A

Profile of Sales Leadership Research

SALES LEADERSHIP RESEARCH (1991–1994)

AchieveGlobal's sales leadership research profiled leading sales organizations in North America, Europe, and Japan. It focused on how customer's expectations and perceptions are changing as well as how outstanding sales organizations are meeting those expectations.

The study involved 300 senior sales executives, sales-training managers, field sales managers, salespeople, and customers of 24 organizations. A pilot study was conducted with 11 sales organizations in Belgium and The Netherlands. Comments made by research participants appear throughout this book.

In each of the companies selected to participate in the study (see Table A-1), we interviewed sales vice presidents, sales directors, field sales managers, salespeople, sales-training directors, and customers of their organizations. The interview questions explored topics such as:

- How are customers changing? How are their challenges, needs, and expectations evolving? What is influencing these changes?
- How is the competitive environment changing? Why is it getting continually harder to maintain a competitive edge?
- What sales strategies are leading sales organizations implementing?
- How will salespeople have to sell differently in the coming decade?
- What do leading sales organizations do to ensure that their salespeople are successful in a changing market?

TABLE A-1
Companies Participating in the Sales Leadership Research[1]

Market	Company	Industry
North America	United States	
	American Airlines	Transportation services
	Hewlett-Packard Company	Computers/high technology
	Northwestern Mutual Life Insurance Company	Insurance
	Scott Paper Company	Paper/forest products
	Xerox Corporation	Office equipment
Europe	France	
	Biscuiterie Nantaise	Foods
	Matra-Hachette	Telecommunications
	Ordo	General manufacturing
	Germany	
	Bayerische Vereinsbank	Financial services
	Boehme Chemie	Health and beauty aids
	Siemens	Semiconductors/electronics
	Belgium	
	N.V. Bekaert	Steel production
	The Netherlands	
	Océ van der Grinten	Office equipment
	Rank Xerox Netherlands	Office equipment
	Sweden	
	Rank Xerox Sweden	Office equipment
	United Kingdom	
	3M	Precision manufacturing
	Allen & Hanbury's	Pharmaceuticals
	Iron Trades Insurance Group	Insurance
	Rank Xerox	Office equipment

(continued)

TABLE A-1
Companies Participating in the Sales Leadership Research[1]—(concluded)

Market	Company	Industry
Pacific Rim	Japan	
	Fuji Xerox Company	Office equipment
	NEC Corporation	Electronics/ semiconductors
	Sony Corporation	Electronics/ semiconductors
	Shiseido Corporation	Cosmetics
	Tokio Marine & Fire Insurance Company	Financial services

[1]The North American companies were recognized by *Sales & Marketing Management* magazine as top performers. The European and Japanese companies were selected because of their extraordinary sales performance and reputation in their local markets.

- How can training, coaching, process, and management enhance the performance of salespeople?
- What attitudes, skills, knowledge, and personal characteristics typify the most outstanding salespeople and sales managers in these companies?

By asking each group similar questions, we were able to capture a variety of points of view. We also interviewed customers who deal with each company to understand the extent to which sales leaders are meeting their expectations and to understand what customers like—and dislike—about salespeople and sales organizations.

COMPANY PROFILES

Allen & Hanbury's (United Kingdom)

Allen & Hanbury's is a manufacturer of pharmaceuticals located in Middlesex, England. It is owned by Glaxo Holdings, the second largest pharmaceutical manufacturer in the world, with worldwide sales of $5.0 billion in 1993.

American Airlines (United States)

American Airlines has the highest revenues of any airline and has been rated best in service among all U.S. carriers. A subsidiary of the AMR Corporation, American Airlines has expanded during the last few years using acquisitions and marketing alliances to develop a stronger international route network. In 1993, operating income was $14.7 billion.

Bayerische Vereinsbank Groupe (Germany)

Bayerische Vereinsbank Groupe is a market-oriented bank based in Munich, Germany. In 1992, they recorded total assets of approximately DM 251 billion, or $147.5 billion.

N.V. Bekaert S.A. (Belgium)

Bekaert, founded in 1880 and located in Kortrijk, Belgium, is a manufacturer of steel, steel wire, steel wire products, and steel cord. It is also involved in engineering and consulting. Sales in 1992 reached approximately BF 53 billion, or $1.6 billion.

Biscuiterie Nantaise (France)

Biscuiterie Nantaise, headquartered in Nantes, France, is a well-established company that manufactures a wide variety of cookies, biscuits, and snacks. It is now a joint venture between U.S.–based Pepsico Foods International, which registered $25 billion in sales in 1993, and General Mills, Inc., with $8.5 billion in sales in 1994. BN is the leader in the markets for *gouterfourrés* cookies and salted snacks and is known for its innovative products and marketing.

Boehme Chemie Gesellschaft (Germany)

Boehme Chemie Gesellschaft, headquartered in Dusseldorf, Germany, produces and distributes detergents and organic and inorganic chemicals such as soap powders, fabric softeners, starches, car care products, adhesives, cosmetics, insecticides, and herbicides. Boehme Chemie is owned by Henkel KGAA, whose sales in 1992 reached $3.2 billion.

Fuji Xerox Company, Ltd. (Japan)

Fuji Xerox, based in Tokyo, Japan, manufactures and markets xerographic copiers and duplicators, and other office equipment. Jointly owned by Rank Xerox Ltd. and Fuji Photo Film Company Ltd., Fuji Xerox recorded 1993 sales at approximately Y 571.9 billion.

Hewlett-Packard Company (United States)

Hewlett-Packard is the world's largest and most diversified manufacturer of electronic measurement and testing equipment and the world's second largest computer workstation manufacturer. Hewlett-Packard, based in Palo Alto, California, offers products that include reduced-instruction-set computing (RISC) minicomputers and computer workstations, networking products, medical electronic equipment, testing and measurement systems, calculators, and chemical analysis systems. In 1993, sales reached $20.3 billion.

Iron Trades Insurance Group (United Kingdom)

Iron Trades Insurance Group is a leading provider of all classes of insurance policy and underwriting services to personal buyers and commercial sectors, via a well-developed network of offices throughout the United Kingdom. Headquartered in London, the company is privately held.

Matra-Hachette (France)

Matra-Hachette is a manufacturer of high-technology communications products. It is a division of Matra S.A., which is a Paris-based defense manufacturer focusing on products such as airborne and land-based weapons, space telecommunications, electronic components, robotics, motor vehicles, and automated urban and interurban transport systems. In 1993, Matra merged with Hachette, creating a new company called Matra-Hachette. In 1992, sales were estimated at FF 55 billion. Matra-Hachette is a subsidiary of Lagardere Groupe holding company.

Minnesota Mining & Manufacturing (3M)
(United Kingdom)

Minnesota Mining & Manufacturing (3M) is a distributor of tape and adhesive products, electronic connectors and devices, surgical and medical supplies, and pharmaceutical and consumer products. The parent company, located in St. Paul, Minnesota, recorded net sales for 1993 at $14.0 billion with approximate sales at $13 billion. The United Kingdom division is headquartered in Berkshire, England.

NEC Corporation (Japan)

NEC is an international supplier of communications systems and equipment, computers, and industrial electronic systems and electron devices. Revenue in 1993 was $30.6 billion or Y 3.5 trillion.

Northwestern Mutual Life Insurance Company (United States)

Northwestern Mutual is the 10th largest life insurance company in the United States, with assets of $44 billion (1993). The Milwaukee, Wisconsin–based company has more than two million policyholders of life and disability insurance and annuities. Northwestern has 4.1 million policies, with more than $224 billion of insurance in force. Northwestern markets its services through a nationwide network of 7200 exclusive agents and operates in all 50 U.S. states and the District of Columbia, with more than 100 general agency offices.

Océ van der Grinten, N.V. (Netherlands)

Océ, founded in 1877 and based in The Netherlands, produces and sells printers and printer supplies, plain-paper copiers, plotters, and overhead films. In 1993, net sales were approximately NG 2.6 billion.

Ordo S.A. (France)

Ordo is the largest manufacturer and distributor of wooden office furniture in France, with 23 percent of the market. Ordo, a French company, was created in 1910 and run by a cabinetmaker, Rene Leveque. Nearly 70 percent of Ordo's employees are cabinetmakers. In 1992, Ordo became part of the Haworth Group (United States). Ordo's sales in 1992 were approximately FF 204 million.

Rank Xerox (United Kingdom)

Rank Xerox, based in Buckinghamshire, England, is jointly owned by Xerox Corporation and the Rank Organization of the United Kingdom. Benefiting from both Xerox, who manufactures repro-graphic and electronic printing systems, and Rank, who manufactures consumer and industrial scientific and electronic equipment, Rank Xerox delivers a full range of document-processing products and services to 80 countries in Europe, Africa, the Middle East, and Asia. Sales in 1992 were registered at £1.9 billion or $3.2 billion.

Scott Paper Company (United States)

Scott Paper Company, located in Philadelphia, Pennsylvania, is the world's leading manufacturer of tissue products, such as toilet paper and paper towels, and one of America's leading producers of coated printing and publishing papers. Scott's commercial division has substantial sales in paper towel systems, cloth replacement wipes, and cleaners. Scott Paper sells its paper and nonwoven fiber products in more than 60 countries, and most of its foreign operations are at least 50 percent locally owned. The commercial division participated in Learning International's study. Scott's 1993 sales totaled $4.7 billion.

Shiseido Company (Japan)

Shiseido Company, a Tokyo, Japan–based firm, is a major manufacturer and exporter of cosmetics and toiletries. Divisions and subsidiaries include Carita, Beaute Prestige International (BPI), Alma Coiffure, and Zotos International. Sales in 1991 reached $3.5 billion, with approximately 16 percent coming from exports.

Siemens (Germany)

Siemens, headquartered in Munich, Germany, develops, manufactures, sells, and services a wide range of systems and products related to the production, distribution, and application of electricity. Uses include power generation, power transmission and distribution, private and public communication systems, defense electronics, and audio and video systems. In 1993, revenues were DM 81.6 billion.

Sony Corporation (Japan)

Sony Corporation, based in Tokyo, Japan, is a world leader in consumer electronics, video technology, recordings, and films, generating approximately 70 percent of its sales outside of Japan. Sony also owns 52.5 percent of audio equipment manufacturer Aiwa. Sony's new hardware technologies include high-definition television and 8-mm video. Net sales in 1993 reached $34.4 billion or Y 3.9 trillion.

The Tokio Marine & Fire Insurance Company (Japan)

The Tokio Marine & Fire Insurance Company is the world's largest property and casualty insurance company. (Japan's property and casualty insurance market is the second largest in the world, after the United States.) Through a domestic network of 529 offices, the company provides marine, fire, casualty, and auto insurance. Assets in 1993 totaled Y 6.8 trillion or $58.9 billion.

Xerox Corporation (United States)

Xerox is the world's leading manufacturer of high-end copiers. The company also makes scanners, printers, and document-processing software. Xerox the document company is committed to redefining the way information, whether in paper or electronic form, moves through corporate offices. Xerox was a 1989 Malcolm Baldrige Award winner. Sales in 1993 were recorded at $16.8 billion.

COMPANIES THAT PARTICIPATED IN THE PILOT PHASE

Following are the 11 companies that participated in the Benelux pilot study:

Name	Industry
Artic	Frozen foods
Avis Fleet Services	Auto fleet leasing
BP Oil International	Petrochemicals
N.V. Bekaert	Steel wire and cord
Gregg	Temporary office services
KN Nederland	Office equipment
Océ	Office equipment
Philip Morris	Cigarettes/tobacco
Schering	Pharmaceuticals
TNT	Air transport
Veldhoven Beheermaatschappij	Textile/apparel

Sales Performance Research Studies from AchieveGlobal

For more information about studies listed in this appendix, please contact:

Research Department
AchieveGlobal Inc.
8875 Hidden River Parkway
Tampa, Florida 33637
(813) 977-8875

DRIVING ISSUES RESEARCH (1998–1999)

AchieveGlobal's survey of sales executives around the world focused on the key issues impacting sales organizations and salespeople today and into the future. The study involved 100 sales organizations and targeted sales executives. The research revealed that sales organizations face challenges related to managing customer relationships over time, attracting and retaining high-performing salespeople, and dealing with more demanding customers.

When respondents were asked to rate the most significant problems they faced in sales management, the top two responses were "customer relations" and "retention of salespeople." A significant portion of the respondents recognized training as a potential solution for retaining and attracting strong salespeople.

SALES LEADERSHIP RESEARCH (1991–1994)

AchieveGlobal's Sales Leadership research, an international study of leading sales organizations in North America, Europe, and Japan, focused on how customers' expectations and perceptions are changing as well as how outstanding sales organizations around the world are meeting those expectations. The study involved 300 senior sales executives, sales-training managers, field sales managers, salespeople, and customers of 24 organizations.

A pilot study was conducted with 11 sales organizations in Belgium and The Netherlands. The research revealed that sales organizations are employing a variety of different sales strategies to develop long-term relationships with customers and adapt to changes in their markets. Aspects of the research were incorporated into the white paper *Sales Coaching: The Key to Leading a High-Performance Sales Team*. Comments made by research participants appear throughout this book.

ROLES OF THE SALESPERSON (1987, 1990, 1994)

AchieveGlobal's Roles of the Salesperson research was conducted to gain an understanding of the characteristics and practices of top-performing salespeople. The two-phased study involved more than 1600 salespeople and sales managers at 33 North American manufacturing and service companies. The research examined the behaviors that distinguish salespeople who are judged to be highly effective by colleagues and customers, as well as by their achievement of quota. It revealed that top-performing salespeople consistently fulfill three roles: strategic orchestrator, business consultant, and long-term ally.

CUSTOMER LOYALTY RESEARCH (1989, 1991–92)

This study identified the factors important to the buyer-seller relationship, with particular focus on determining why customers sever relationships with supplier organizations. Through focus groups and telephone interviews with more than 200 buyers in seven industries in North America, six factors were uncovered:

- Business expertise and image

- Dedication to the customer
- Account sensitivity and guidance
- Product performance and quality
- Service department excellence
- Confirmation of capabilities

The first three have the greatest impact on overall customer satisfaction and rely heavily on the salesperson's skill and involvement before, during, and after the sale, highlighting the pivotal role a salesperson plays in building customer loyalty. This research served as the basis for the *Profiles in Customer Loyalty* white paper.

After the North American study was conducted, the research was replicated in 12 countries in North America, Europe, and the Pacific Rim in 1991 and 1992. The European research served as the basis for the white paper *Achieving Customer Loyalty in Europe.*

SALES PRODUCTIVITY (1990)

In 1990, AchieveGlobal conducted research to identify the management activities that have the most critical effect on sales productivity. Information was gathered through telephone interviews with 300 sales executives in a variety of industries as well as through focus groups with sales executives in United States and Canadian companies.

Although 10 activities were identified as having a major effect on sales productivity, the following three activities have the greatest impact:

- Building long-term relationships with clients
- Providing salespeople with in-depth knowledge of the company's products or services
- Maintaining a positive image of their organization in the marketplace

This study served as the basis for the white paper *Sales Productivity Action Planning Guide.*

SERVICE EXCELLENCE (1990)

The Service Excellence research examined the philosophies, strategies, and service employee competencies that characterize top service organizations. Interviews were conducted with front-line service employees, service managers, general managers, and customers in 14 U.S. companies recognized for their focus on providing outstanding customer service.

Based on these interviews, AchieveGlobal identified several common philosophies and practices that foster superior customer relations: collecting feedback from customers to assess their needs, empowering frontline service employees to better serve the customer, emphasizing continuous service improvement, and involving senior managers in customer service.

In addition, the study determined that service-minded organizations hire, develop, and motivate their service personnel to be skilled in 15 "master competencies," ranging from building customer loyalty and confidence to using effective interpersonal skills. This research served as the basis for the *Lessons from Top Service Providers* white paper.

SALES FORCE TURNOVER (1989)

This study examined sales-force turnover in an effort to identify the reasons salespeople leave their jobs and to assess what managers can do to improve sales-force retention. Conducted through telephone interviews with 337 sales managers and 165 salespeople selected randomly from major U.S. and Canadian firms, the research revealed that sales-force turnover occurred at an annual rate of approximately 27 percent, costing the average company up to $200,000.

A key finding of the study was that high sales-force turnover can be avoided through a systematic management strategy to provide salespeople with the fundamentals they need to perform their jobs effectively. This study served as the basis for the white paper *What Does Sales Force Turnover Cost You?*

ROLES OF THE SALES MANAGER (1987)

This study identified the critical behaviors of effective sales managers, based on 2500 written questionnaires completed by 187 managers and selected colleagues, subordinates, and superiors in 20 private and public North American organizations. The research revealed that sales managers can improve their productivity by developing their ability in three key roles: strategist, communicator, and mentor. In addition, highly effective sales managers must consistently fulfill all three roles. This research served as the basis for AchieveGlobal's *Challenges of Sales Management* program.

SALES AND MARKETING TRENDS (1987)

A 1987 study of sales and marketing trends commissioned by AchieveGlobal identified key factors that have an impact on the sales function in 10 high-growth industries. Interviews with 135 senior sales and marketing executives from 80 organizations revealed 10 key trends that affect the sales environment:

- Increasing competition
- Consolidated buying groups
- Broader, more diverse product/service lines
- Technological breakthroughs
- Elongated sales cycles
- Shortened product life cycles
- Increasing customer sophistication
- Service orientation
- Deregulation
- Customer demand-driven selling environment

These research findings were confirmed in a 1989 follow-up study conducted in the high technology and financial service industries.

Appendix C

Customer Loyalty Research

AchieveGlobal's Customer Loyalty research identified factors important to the buyer-seller relationship, with particular focus on determining why customers sever relationships with supplier organizations. The same expectations ranked as the top 10 in three markets—North America, Europe, and Japan. The complete list of expectations is shown here.

A product or service that:

- Is priced competitively.
- Has a high level of technical support.
- Has support in product application/usage.
- Allows purchasing specific features.
- Is delivered on time.
- Performs as anticipated.
- Is compatible with products and services purchased.
- Is not quickly obsolete.

A salesperson who:

- Knows his or her competition.
- Wants business.
- Brings in others to meet needs.
- Is honest.
- Has a pleasant personality.
- Helps customer solve problems.
- Knows his or her products and services.
- Is backed by his or her own company.
- Provides a total package.

- Helps the customer be successful.
- Anticipates problems.
- Suggests creative solutions.
- Provides guidance.
- Instills confidence.
- Presents products understandably.
- Meets customers' emergency needs.
- Keeps promises.
- Takes a long-term perspective.
- Helps sell recommendations.
- Lets the customer know of changes.
- Has a good personal appearance.
- Can be reached when needed.
- Responds to customer concerns.
- Acknowledges product/service weaknesses.
- Understands business and economic trends.
- Understands decision-making process.
- Helps the customer provide better products and services.
- Works to develop a smarter way of doing business.

A supplier organization that:

- Has a name recognized in the marketplace.
- Has a good reputation in the marketplace.
- Projects awareness of social responsibility.
- Is associated with high-quality products and services.
- Has high-caliber management.
- Is financially stable.
- Has been in business for a long time.
- Is associated with innovation.
- Adapts to changes in the marketplace.
- Allows on-site inspection.
- Provides customer references.
- Can be trusted.

Customer service providers who:

- Are sensitive to the customer's needs.

- Have the customer's best interest in mind.
- Are dependable.
- Ask appropriate questions for information.
- Pay attention to what the customer says.
- Are always willing to help.
- Understand customer concerns.
- Are courteous.
- Are knowledgeable.
- Indicate plans to help the customer.
- Explain when services will be performed.
- Provide prompt service.
- Are easily accessible.
- Solve customers' problems.
- Make the customer feel confident in business dealings.

The Consultative Salesperson: Knowledge, Skills, Attitudes, and Personal Characteristics

This appendix lists the knowledge, skills, attitudes, and personal characteristics necessary for conducting the practices associated with the roles of strategic orchestrator, business consultant, and long-term ally. A needs analysis within your own organization would reveal which of these are most important for your business.

Knowledge of:

- Your company's products and services
  Applications
  How they can be combined to best meet your customer's needs
- Competitive products and services
  Communicates the advantages and disadvantages
  How they compare with your own products and services
  Under what conditions they might be recommended

- General business knowledge
  How businesses work
  General business, industry, and economic trends
- Your company
  Your sales strategy
  Functions and capabilities of various departments, teams, groups, and individuals and how they can add value
  Your company's policies and procedures

Skills:

- Research skills

  Uncovers the customer's business, products and services competition, industry, culture, organization

  Reads annual reports and other current information

  Accesses databases

  Identifies the customer's decision-making process

- Communication skills

  Listens actively

  Demonstrates understanding

  Expresses ideas clearly and logically

  Probes effectively; asks insightful questions

  Interviews people throughout the customer organization

  Persuades

  Gains commitment

  Develops and delivers formal and informal presentations

  Presents a professional image, verbally and nonverbally

  Expresses ideas well verbally, in person and by phone

  Writes clearly and succinctly

- Self-management skills

  Builds effective networks

  Uses time and territory effectively

  Gathers feedback, and identifies ways to be more productive

- Problem-solving and planning skills

  Identifies needs and challenges

  Gathers relevant information

  Analyzes data and draws appropriate conclusions

  Generates creative solutions

  Assesses alternative solutions

  Makes decisions

  Makes appropriate recommendations

- Organization skills

  Organizes information

  Performs precall analyses

Prepares for sales call

Organizes information after sales call

- Team skills

Identifies situations where a team approach is appropriate

Puts together ad hoc teams

Delegates responsibility

Leads teams

Organizes activities of team members

Tracks progress of teams

Uses support systems

- Financial skills

Calculates financial impact of recommendations and various
activities

Oversees invoicing

- Negotiation skills

Plans for negotiations

Negotiates solutions in which the customer, salesperson,
and sales organization all win

- Interpersonal skills

Demonstrates appropriate humor

Demonstrates consideration for the customer's time

Makes others feel comfortable and important

Is accessible; responds quickly to requests

Credits others for ideas

Doesn't pressure the customer

- Maintains relationships
- Provides added-value information, ideas, and services

Attitudes and Personal Characteristics:

- Intelligence

Learns quickly

Absorbs vast amounts of information

Is able to sort out important information from unimportant
information

- Commitment

Continues own education and self-improvement

Helps customers achieve short-term and long-term business objectives

- Customer-focused approach

Does what is right for the customer

"Keeps an eye out" for the customer—even when not doing business

Stays interested

- Proactive approach

Looks for opportunities instead of waiting to react

Is assertive; asks for business

Takes initiative

Asks for feedback

- Credibility and integrity

Is honest—acknowledges limitations and admits mistakes

Stands up for beliefs

Demonstrates integrity under all circumstances

Only promises what the company can deliver

Communicates genuine interest and concern through words and actions

Is tactful and responsible

Keeps confidential information confidential

Never criticizes others in his or her own organization

- Thoroughness

Looks after the details

Follows through consistently

- Common sense
- Reliability

Completes projects and delivers things on time

Is prompt for appointments

- Flexibility, adaptability

Alters plans, arrangements, and activities according to customers' changing needs

Is willing to give up preconceived notions

- Optimism
  Believes in the value of products and services
  Has a winning attitude
  Sees competition and problems as opportunities
  to demonstrate excellence
  Takes competitive losses gracefully
  Sees failure or rejection as an opportunity to learn
- Energy level
  Works hard
  Constantly looks for new opportunities
- Ambition
  Sets challenging personal goals
  Sets and follows a career path
  Commits to excellence
- Motivation
  Sets high goals
  Seeks nonfinancial rewards
  Has a strong work ethic

Appendix E

The High Performance Salesperson—From the Customer's Point of View

While doing the research for this book, we had the opportunity to speak to a number of insightful customers. Here's what they say about the knowledge, skills, attitudes, and personal characteristics of the "quintessential" salesperson:

Knowledge

"The level of competence demanded of salespeople will take quantum leaps. They need to be more professional, more clever, and have more technical knowledge because the customer base is more sophisticated about business."

—Customer, Scott Paper Company (United States)

Skills

"Salespeople should not focus on what they want to sell but must sell to the needs."

—Customer, American Airlines (United States)

"They sell from the top down; they get as high as they can in the organization to find someone who understands how the products are used and what the cost and use issues are."

—Customer, Scott Paper Company (United States)

"They think logically; they base decisions on facts and data."

—Customer, Tokio Marine & Fire Insurance Company (Japan)

"Once they understand a problem, they own it."

—Customer, American Airlines (United States)

"To be successful in sales, you need to be an intelligent listener. . . Most sales-people, however, are like alligators—they have great big mouths, little eyes, and little ears."

—Customer, Scott Paper Company (United States)

"They help me make good decisions and give me the tools to defend my decision within my company."

—Customer, Océ (The Netherlands)

"They ask questions to uncover the priorities, but it feels like a conversation in the living room with your best friend."

—Customer, Scott Paper Company (United States)

"Salespeople have to be better at everything than they used to be—more technically knowledgeable, good negotiators, good problem solvers. There is also a trend toward salespeople offering a more complete service to customers; more of an entrepreneur. . . than a salesperson."

—Customer, 3M (United Kingdom)

"If salespeople are going to grow the business, they need to be able to keep lots of balls in the air. Otherwise the business will plateau. So, good organizational skills are critical."

—Customer, Scott Paper Company (United States)

Attitudes and Personal Characteristics

"After a long negotiation, he lost out on a large deal. He took it very well, and we continued after that loss on a professional basis. This surprised me. He was a good loser, and he remained a professional."

—Customer, Océ (The Netherlands)

"They have to become broad in their vision. Stop short-term thinking and build the long-term relationship. It's crucial."

—Customer, Océ (The Netherlands)

"The salesperson must build the customer's confidence . . . find a solution in order to reassure the buyer, and prove one's good intentions."

—Customer, Matra (France)

"They must fulfill promises. Even when the company they work for doesn't keep promises, I still hold them liable."

—Customer, Océ (The Netherlands)

"You can build a house on what they promise."

—Customer, BP Oil (Benelux)

"Not sticking to your promises ends the relationship, as far as I'm concerned."

—Customer, Philip Morris (Belgium)

"Integrity is the umbrella I find crucial."

Customer, Océ (The Netherlands)

"If there is a complaint, they listen to what you have to say, and then take action quickly."

—Customer, Iron Trades Insurance (United Kingdom)

"Have a genuine, helpful, caring attitude."

—Customer, American Airlines (United States)

"If you can't meet expectations, don't sell."

—Customer, Gregg (Benelux)

Appendix F

Glossary

Best practice. The best known procedures or activities that can be used to achieve a desired outcome.

Business consultant. A salesperson who fosters customer confidence and strengthens selling relationships by demonstrating:

- General business knowledge
- A comprehensive understanding of the customer's business challenges
- An ability to develop and help implement effective solutions and recommendations

Campaign Management Software. An application that helps marketers plan, execute, evaluate, and refine marketing programs.

CD-ROM business card. The size of a credit card, these can be printed with typical business information, but they also store information in any combination of text, graphics, photos, audio, video, documents, spreadsheets, presentations, and links to e-mail or Websites. They work in the CD-ROM drives on both PC and Macintosh platforms.

Computer-Telephony Integration. The convergence of two once-separate technologies—computing and telephony—and the most vital application service for next generation customer relationship solutions. CTI links your telephony resources, such as automated call distribution and your interactive voice response (IVR) system with your corporate information infrastructure.

Consultative selling. The process of helping the customer achieve strategic goals through the use of your product or service.

Creative problem solving. The ability to develop and combine non-traditional alternatives to meet the specific needs of the situation.

Customer Management. Automates all the activities that an organization may have with its customers, including sales, telesales, marketing, telemarketing, customer service, and the help desk.

Customer Relationship Process (CRP). The sequence of activities performed by the people who are in direct contact with customers that enable the supplier organization to meet or exceed customer requirements.

Database Management. Managing and synchronizing data stored in various databases to flow seamlessly and easily across the entire enterprise.

Data Mart. A type of data warehouse designed primarily to address a specific function or department's needs, as opposed to a data warehouse, which is traditionally meant to address the needs of the organization from an enterprise perspective.

Data Mining. Extracting hidden predictive information from large databases and automatically detecting trends and associations hidden in data. Using a combination of machine learning, statistical analysis, modeling techniques, and database technology, data mining finds patterns and subtle relationships in data and infers rules that allow the prediction of future results. Typical applications include market segmentation, customer profiling, fraud detection, evaluation of retail promotions, and credit risk analysis.

Data Warehouse. A system for storing and delivering massive quantities of data. Data warehouse software often includes sophisticated compression techniques for fast searches, as well as advanced filtering. A data warehouse is often remote so researchers can use it freely without slowing down day-to-day operations of the production database. Front-end decision support tools are used to access the data to produce useful information for selling, marketing, and servicing customers.

Enterprise Resource Planning (ERP). Positioned as the foundation and integration of enterprisewide information systems, this is sometimes described as the organization's IT "backbone." It provides users with the ability to interact with a common corporate database for a comprehensive range of applications managing financial, asset, and cost accounting; production operations and materials; personnel; plants; and archived documents.

Executive Information System. Analyzes performance, develops marketing plans, performs sales forecasting, and manages human resources.

Ideal business relationship. A business relationship characterized by a sense of rapport, trust, and respect between the salesperson and customer, with the expectation that their organizations will do business over the long term and in a mutually beneficial way.

Interactive voice response (IVR). A system that allows simple tasks to be executed either through touch-tone input or speech recognition, without the assistance of a live agent. This results in instant access to information for callers and greater call-handling capacity for companies, without additional staffing. Fax-on-demand is a natural next step. A customer can call an agent or an IVR system and retrieve sales literature, directions to a retail outlet, and price lists instantly and automatically by fax.

Internet. The world's largest TCP/IP network. Transmission control protocol/Internet protocol is a networking standard that forms the basis for the Internet, which has become a worldwide system of interconnected computer networks. The Internet is built on a series of protocols such as TCP/IP, HTTP, HTML, and FTP to provide an easy and powerful exchange of data and information.

Intranet. An internal system of connected networks built on Internet protocols and usually connected to the Internet via a firewall, that is, a computer insulating the internal network from the Internet. It allows only qualified traffic to pass in and out.

Knowledge Management. Represents a more humanistic approach to business process redesign than reengineering. Prescribed changes may be no less radical, but they use the organization's own assets to identify and correct process flaws. KM calls for equipping an organization with enterprise systems, interpersonal tools and mobile devices to integrate human insight with computer-processing power to measure results and provide continuous feedback. By applying knowledge, workers add their own contribution to it. KM's emphasis on revenue growth helps to foster worker buy-in.

Life-Cycle Management. The practice of tracking a customer through every stage of a relationship: initial contact, proposal, contract negotiation, commitment, delivery, installation, feedback, and, ideally, repeat sale.

Long-term ally. Salesperson who demonstrates commitment—and is able to contribute—to the customer's immediate- and long-term success throughout the entire Customer Relationship Process.

Loyal customer. A buyer who chooses to do business with a particular supplier and intends to buy from that supplier in the future.

Marketing Encyclopedia. A comprehensive database or collection of all current marketing and sales materials in an electronic format available via intranet, the Internet, or CD-ROM. Salespeople can use it to create customized presentations by selecting and organizing material. Content can include presentations, proposals, brochures, catalogs, service manuals, images, videos, and CAD drawings.

Sales coaching. A sequence of conversations and activities that provides ongoing feedback and encouragement to a salesperson or sales team member with the goal of improving that person's performance.

Sales Configurator. Allows salespeople to compare specifications and put together products, while providing pricing and identifying possible problems in production.

Sales executive. Sales vice presidents and directors of sales.

Sales Force Automation. Software and hardware that helps qualify leads and keeps contact information about existing accounts. It maintains the history of clients and lets managers track salespeople's activities. SFA may include contact managers, marketing encyclopedias, sales configuration, and order-entry tools, but generally is designed for workflow applications.

Sales strategy. The sales organization's role in adding value, meeting customer expectations, and differentiating from competition.

Sales training. The process of providing a salesperson or sales team member with the skills, knowledge, and attitudes necessary to increase that person's productivity.

Satisfied customer. A buyer who buys from a particular supplier, but expects to buy from others in the future.

SPPM. Sales Performance Process Map; a subset of the Customer Relationship Process, focusing solely on the sales function.

Strategic orchestrator. A salesperson who coordinates all of the information, resources, and activities needed to support customers before, during, and after the sale.

Strategic sales coaching. The use of sales coaching to achieve a sales strategy in a systematic way.

Strategic sales training. The use of sales training to achieve a sales strategy in a systematic way.

Supply Chain Management Software. Identifies a company's business constraints through the supply chain, the series of process and suppliers that move products from raw materials to the arms of the customer. It helps salespeople make sure they can deliver a profitable product to a customer on time.

Synchronization. Applications that bring information from your legacy databases to agents' desktops as customer calls arrive or coordinate the updating of data on different databases.

Team selling. When a team from the supplier organization meets with a potential or existing customer with the intention of advancing a sales cycle and building a business relationship.

Telemarketing/Telesales. Integrates with telephony or communications equipment such as ACD (automated call distributors) or IVR (integrated voice recognition) devices to support telephone sales efforts.

Workflow Management Software. Trains, organizes, and equips your sales team to function collaboratively—sharing information, knowledge, and information.

Bibliography

AchieveGlobal. *Profiles in Customer Loyalty,* 1989 and *Achieving Customer Loyalty in Europe,* 1992.

AchieveGlobal. *Sales Productivity Action Planning Guide,* 1992.

AchieveGlobal. "Sales Productivity in the 1990s." Preliminary Report, 1990, p. 9.

Cespedes, Frank V., Stephen X. Doyle, and Robert J. Freedman. "Teamwork for Today's Selling." *Harvard Business Review,* March/April 1989, pp. 44–58.

Davis, Jeffrey. "Are You Next?" *Business 2.0,* March 1999. (*http://www.business2.com/articles/1999/03/content/coverstory.html*)

Deutsch, Claudia H. "Software That Can Make a Grown Company Cry." *New York Times,* Money and Business/Financial Desk, November 8, 1998.

Fay, Christopher. "Royalties from Loyalties." *Journal of Business Strategy* 15, no. 2, March/April 1994, pp. 47–51.

Graham, John R. "Capturing the Cyber Customer." Section: vol. 43, no. 11, *American,* Nov. 1998, p. 9.

Hayes, and S. W. Harley, "How Buyers View Industrial Salespeople." *Industrial Marketing Management* 18, 1989, pp. 73–80.

Herrington, Mike. "What Does a Customer Want?" *Across the Board,* The Conference Board, 1993.

Howard, James S. "Suppliers and Customers Put Down the Gloves." *D & B Reports* 41, no. 3, May/June 1992, pp. 26–28.

Jolson, Marvin A., Alan J. Dubinsky, et al. "Transforming the Sales Force with Leadership." *Sloan Management Review,* Spring 1993, pp. 95–106.

Journal of Business and Industrial Marketing 8, no. 4 (1993).

Keenan, William, Jr. "Death of the Sales Manager." *Sales & Marketing Management,* April 1998.

King, James P. "Union Pacific Gets Back on Track with Training." *Training and Development,* August 1993, pp. 30–37.

Kirkpatrick, D. L. "Techniques for Evaluating Training Programs." *Training Director's Journal*, November 1959.

Learning International. *Achieving Customer Loyalty in Europe.* White paper, 1992.

Learning International. *Exchange*, no. 36, 1991, p. 3.

Learning International. *Profiles in Customer Loyalty.* White paper, 1989.

Learning International. *Sales Productivity Action Planning Guide.* White paper, 1992.

Learning International. "Sales Productivity in the 1990s." Preliminary report, 1990, p. 9.

Linsalata, Ralph, and Richard Highland. "Reengineering the Selling Process." White paper. Waltham, MA: Eavoiy Systems Corporation.

Magrath, Allan J. "From the Practitioners Desk: A Comment on Personal Selling and Sales Management in the New Millennium." *Journal of Personal Selling and Sales Management*, vol. XVII, no. 1, Winter 1997, pp. 45–47.

O'Connell, William A., and William Keenan, Jr. "The Shape of Things to Come." *Sales and Marketing Management Magazine*, January 1990, p. 38.

PC Week, June 15, 1998.

Porter, Michael E. *The Competitive Advantage of Nations.* New York: The Free Press, 1990.

Reichheld, Frederick F. "The Loyalty Effect." *Harvard Business School Press*, Boston, 1996, p. 37.

Reichheld, Frederick F. W., and Earl Sasser, Jr. "Zero Defections: Quality Comes to Service." *Harvard Business Review*, September/October 1990, p. 301.

Retchfeld, Barry. *Personal Selling Power 13*, no. 6, September 1993, pp. 26–33.

Robbins, Chris. "Successful Selling in the Corporate Jungle." *American Salesman*, April 1998.

Sager, Ira. "The Few, the True, the Blue." *Business Week*, May 30, 1994, p. 124.

Sales & Marketing Management, April/May/June 1998.

Sales and Marketing Management's 1998 Productivity Study. Dysart, Joe. *Custom Made Selling Power* Jan./Feb., 1999, pp. 87–88.

Stalk, George Jr., and Thomas M. Hout. *Competing against Time.* New York: The Free Press, 1990.

Standard & Poor's Industry Surveys. *Health Care Products and Services,* September 9, 1993, p. 39.

Steinbrink, Jon P. "How to Pay Your Sales Force." Steinbrink, *Harvard Business Review,* July/Aug. 1978, p. 111.

Treacy, Michael; and Fred Wiersema. "Customer Intimacy and Other Value Disciplines." *Harvard Business Review,* January/February 1993, pp. 84–93.

Vinchur, A. J., Schippmann, F. S. Switzer, III, and P. L. Roth. "A Meta-Analytic Review of Predictors of Job Performance for Salespeople." *Journal of Applied Psychology,* vol. 83, no. 4, pp. 586–597.

Stevens, Howard. "Smart Hiring: How to Avoid the Most Common Sales Hiring Errors." *Selling Power,* September 1998. pp. 23–26.

Wexley, K. N., and G. P. Lathaam. *Developing and Training Human Resources in Organizations.* New York: HarperCollins, 1991.

Index

Authors

Darlene M. Coker

Darlene Coker manages the AchieveGlobal's Sales Performance product line, studying trends in sales performance, and ensuring that AchieveGlobal's products and services reflect cutting-edge thought leadership in selling.

Darlene has written and developed training programs in the fields of sales, professional presentation skills and project management, and has a background in sales, training, and consulting.

Her articles and papers and ideas on Sales, Project Management, and Total Quality Management have been presented at industry conferences and in trade publications, and she has lectured at Temple University and the Wharton School of Business.

Edward R. Del Gaizo

Ed Del Gaizo is senior consultant at AchieveGlobal, working with clients primarily in the areas of alternative learning systems and sales performance. Having been director of research for more than a decade at AchieveGlobal, he designed and directed research studies that are the foundation of this book. He is the principal author of the book *The Alligator Trap: How to Sell without Being Turned into a Pair of Shoes*, which provides practical strategies and tips for sales success from top performing salespeople.

Kathleen A. Murray

Kathleen Murray is vice president of Europe and the Middle East for AchieveGlobal. She leads the ongoing development of Achieve-Global's growth in the European, Middle Eastern, and Northern African markets by assisting affiliate partners to develop their business and grow successfully; and by creating new country operations in these markets.

In April 1984, Ms. Murray became the youngest recipient of the President's Achievement Award for extraordinary contribution to the Xerox Corporation.

Sandra L. Edwards

Sandra Edwards is AchieveGlobal's vice-president of International Business Development and Global Accounts. In this role she is responsible for the establishment, development, and execution of AchieveGlobal's knowledge transfer initiative, known as the Institute of Development. The Institute supports growth opportunities and capability enhancement for AchieveGlobal's Affiliate Partners throughout the world. Ms. Edwards also leads the management of the Global Accounts Team.

With over 17 years of experience in sales, consulting, training, management, strategic planning, and business development, Ms. Edwards is an accomplished speaker and sales performance consultant.